International Perspectives of Crime Prevention

Contributions from the 1st Annual International Forum

Eds.
Marc Coester and Erich Marks

with contributions from:
Detlef Otto Bönke, Janina Czapska, Libor Gašpierik, Angelos Giannakopoulos, Elizabeth Johnston, Konstadinos Maras, Jana Müllerová, Anna Karina Nickelsen, Lubomíra Pecková, Tobias Plate, Sławomir Redo, Tiina Ristmäe, Margaret Shaw, Dirk Tänzler

Forum Verlag Godesberg GmbH 2008

Bibliographical Information from the German Library

This publication is recorded in the German Library in the German National Bibliography; detailed bibliographical data can be found on the internet under **http://dnb.ddb.de**

© Forum Verlag Godesberg GmbH,
Mönchengladbach.
All rights reserved.
Mönchengladbach 2008

Produced by: Books on Demand GmbH, Norderstedt
Printed in Germany

Print layout: Marc Coester
Copy-Editor: Giles Ekblom

Cover design: Konstantin Megas, Mönchengladbach

ISBN 978-3-936999-47-1

Content

Introduction 1

Lectures from the 1st Annual International Forum

SŁAWOMIR REDO
Six United Nations guiding principles to make crime prevention work 5

MARGARET SHAW
Why Youth Are Essential Partners in Crime Prevention: An International View 23

ELIZABETH JOHNSTON
The multiple Challenges of Youth facing Violence 37

DETLEF OTTO BÖNKE AND TOBIAS PLATE
Crime Prevention Activities from the Perspective of the German Presidency
of the European Union 43

Contributions from participants at the 1st Annual International Forum

TIINA RISTMÄE
Neighbourhood Watch as an effective crime prevention method in Estonia 53

ANNA KARINA NICKELSEN
Crime Prevention in Denmark - Current status 63

JANINA CZAPSKA
Crime prevention in Poland 18 years after the transformation 71

LIBOR GAŠPIERIK AND JANA MÜLLEROVÁ
Criminological aspects of delinquency of juvenile and criminality of teenage
offenders in the Slovak Republic 85

LUBOMÍRA PECKOVÁ
Crime prevention Strategy in the Slovak Republic 91

ANGELOS GIANNAKOPOULOS, KONSTADINOS MARAS AND DIRK TÄNZLER
Research Findings on Perceptions of Corruption in Seven European Countries
within the EU-Project 'Crime and Culture' 99

WIESBADEN DECLARATION OF THE 12TH GERMAN CRIME PREVENTION
CONGRESS "A STRONG YOUTH – A STRONG FUTURE" 125

Introduction

The **German Congress on Crime Prevention** is an annual event that has taken place since 1995 in different German cities and targets all areas of crime prevention: Administration, the health system, youth welfare, the judiciary, churches, local authorities, the media, politics, the police, crime prevention committees, projects, schools, organisations, associations and science. The desired effect is to present and strengthen crime prevention within a broad societal framework. Thus it contributes to crime reduction as well as to the prevention and the reduced risk of becoming a victim as well as fear of crime. The main objectives of the congress are:

1   Presenting and exchanging current and basic questions of crime prevention and its effectiveness.
2   Bringing together partners within the field of crime prevention.
3   Functioning as a forum for the practice, and fostering the exchange of experiences.
4   Helping to get contacts at an international level and to exchange information.
5   Discussing implementation strategies.
6   Developing and disseminating recommendations for practice, politics, administration and research.

The 2007 12th congress took place on the 18th and 19th June in Wiesbaden (Capital of the State of Hesse) and gathered together more than 2000 people from the field of crime prevention. The discussion focused on the main topic 'Strong Youth – Strong Future' with lectures, an exhibition (with over 120 exhibitors), open forum, internet forum, university for children, a poster session, film forum and other events.

Since its foundation the German Congress on Crime Prevention has been opened to an international audience with a growing number of non-German speaking participants joining. Because prevention is more than a national concern and should be focused internationally this step seemed crucial. Bringing together not only German scientists and practitioners but also international experts in crime prevention and therefore developing a trans-national forum to foster the exchange of knowledge and experience constitutes the main focus of this approach. To give the international guests their own discussion forum, the 1st **Annual International Forum (AIF)** within the German Congress on Crime Prevention took place in 2007. For non-German guests this event offered five AIF lectures in English language as well as other activities that were translated simultaneously. International guests were also able to play an active role by presenting a poster or displaying information within the exhibition.

The programme of the 1st Annual International Forum included:
Dr. Slawomir Redo (United Nations Office on Drugs and Crime, Vienna – UNODC): *For Urban Crime Prevention in Sub-Sahara: United Nations Crime Prevention Guidelines at work*

Dr. Margaret Shaw (International Centre for the Prevention of Crime, Montreal – ICPC. Director of Analysis and Exchange): *Why Youth are Essential Partners in Crime Prevention: an International View*

Elizabeth Johnston (European Forum for Urban Safety Paris – EFUS. Deputy Director): *The multiple Challenges of Youth facing Violence*

Dr. Sohail Husain (Analytical Consulting Services Ltd Hampshire. Director): *Developing Effective Crime Prevention Programmes*

Otto Bönke (German Federal Ministry of Justice, Berlin. Head of Section) **and Dr. Tobias Plate** (German Federal Ministry of the Interior, Berlin. Desk Officer): *Crime Prevention Activities from the Perspective of the German EU-Presidency*

Over the next few years – especially the 2nd and 3rd June 2008 when the 13th German Congress on Crime Prevention as well as the 2nd Annual international Forum take place in Leipzig – we intend to develop this concept further. It is our wish to build an international forum for crime prevention that ensures a competent exchange of ideas, theories and applied approaches.

This book reflects the input and output of the 1st Annual International Forum in 2007. Firstly four lectures of the AIF are printed, followed by contributions from participants of the congress. The articles reflect worldwide views on crime prevention as well as the current status, discussion, research and projects in crime prevention from different countries like Estonia, Denmark, Poland, Germany or the Slovak Republic. The topics range from what works in crime prevention, youth and prevention, youth violence, Neighbourhood Watch and corruption. At the end the Wiesbaden Declaration is included, a report about the key findings of the Wiesbaden congress.

We hope to find a broad audience, interested in the upcoming events of the Annual International Forum as well as the German Congress on Crime Prevention. For more information visit please visit our homepage at http://www.gcocp.org.

Marc Coester and Erich Marks

Lectures from the 1st Annual International Forum

Sławomir Redo[1]

Six United Nations guiding principles to make crime prevention work

"Crime prevention cannot implement itself"

Introduction

The origins of the United Nations' crime prevention movement can be traced back to the late 1980s. At that time, the Organisation started to stress the issue of informal crime prevention systems as of equal importance and complimentary to the operations of law enforcement and criminal justice systems in facilitating the State's protection from crime. Thirty five years after the adoption of the first legal instrument (the Standard Minimum Rules for the Treatment of Prisoners, 1955), the United Nations, realising that the traditional criminal justice systems alone were failing to combat crime, started adopting new instruments, like the Guidelines for the Prevention of Juvenile Delinquency ("The Riyadh Guidelines", General Assembly resolution 45/112, Annex), which focus on young people - the resource and promise of future generations.

Those Guidelines promote the idea that formal systems of control are to be complemented by society's informal social controls. They include a range of measures to be taken by those responsibe, like parents, schools and religious bodies to educate children and young people to respect laws, to regulate the conduct of people as they go about their daily lives and to afford protection to people and property through routine precautions and security measures. The informal and formal systems of control depend upon each other for effectiveness.

In 1997, the General Assembly adopted another crime prevention resolution 51/60 – the "Declaration on Crime and Public Safety" and in the same year the Economic and Social Council (ECOSOC) adopted the resolution 1997/28 on "Firearm regulation for the purposes of crime prevention and public health and safety". However, the most technically viable instruments which have been adopted and evidently pursued by Member States, have entered the United Nations agenda through two other ECOSOC resolutions[2].

---

[1] Doctor of Law; United Nations Office on Drugs and Crime (UNODC), Justice and Integrity Unit, Division for Operation (Vienna, Austria). The views contained in this article do not necessarily reflect the views of the United Nations Secretariat. [From the Editors: Author of three books, co-editor of three books. He published about 45 articles on various crime prevention and criminal justice issues, mostly covered by the United Nations treaty and customary law].

[2] The use and application of only some United Nations soft law instruments are monitored periodically by the surveys of the Secretary-General. For the legislative background of the implementation mechanism see: The Application of United Nations Standards and Norms in Criminal Justice, Expert Group Meeting, Peace Academy, Castle Schlaining, Stadtschlaining, Burgenland, Austria, 10-12 February 2003, United Nations Office on

In 1995, the ECOSOC focussed on crime prevention through the lens of urbanisation, and in 2002 took a comprehensive look at crime prevention in general. Accordingly the ECOSOC adopted two new resolutions: "Guidelines for the Prevention of Urban Crime" (resolution 1995/9, Annex), and "Guidelines for the Prevention of Crime" (resolution 2002/13, Annex). They are both the outcome of intergovernmental and cross-national contributions to the incipient United Nations movement towards more operational and successful crime prevention on a global scale.

Against the background explaining why and how this incipient movement has been shaped, this article presents altogether six United Nations guiding principles to make crime prevention work[3]:

I.   the principle of the rule of law;
II.   the principle of socio-economic inclusion;
III.   the principle of community-centred action;
IV.   the principle of partnership;
V.   the principle of sustainability and accountability; and
VI.   the principle of evidence-based practice.

In the presentation of these six principles, the paper also draws on the additional research contributions to humane and effective crime prevention[4]. Some of them are connected with other United Nations developments that gave those principles their policy and operational context in which they function, but all the contributions explain their rationale.

Drugs and Crime, Vienna, Austria, http://www.unodc.org/pdf/crime/publications/standards%20&%20norms.pdf. In 2004-2007, ECOSOC through its resolutions on the United Nations standards and norms in crime prevention and criminal justice has mandated the UNODC to carry out a number of such surveys, including the 2002 ECOSOC guidelines (see doc. E/CN 15/2007/11, Report of the Secretary-General on United Nations standards and norms in crime prevention and criminal justice). The law-making mechanism of such "soft law" instruments and their impact on domestic legislation and practice is analysed in: Sławomir Redo, United Nations Criminal Justice Norms and Standards and Customary Law", (in:) The Contributions of Specialised Institutes and Non-Governmental Organizations to the United Nations Criminal Justice Program, ed. by M. Cherif Bassiouni, The Hague, Martinus Nijhoff Publishers 1995, pp. 109-135, and in: Impacto de los principios de las Naciones Unidas en la reforma penal, (in:) Congreso Internacional: Las Ciencias Penales en el Siglo XXI, Instituto Nacional de Ciencias Penales, México, 2004, pp. 469-490.

[3] They are conceptualised and synthesised here on the basis of a much larger set of principles provided in both guidelines, developed with partly different legislative drafting techniques. While consolidating them, this article seeks to answer the calls of crime prevention experts to prioritise them, make their presentation more succinct, topical and compact, so as to facilitate their promotion and putting into field operation.

[4] E.g., Erich Marks, Anja Meyer, Ruth Linssen, The Beccaria-project: quality management in crime prevention, (in:) Erich Marks, Anja Meyer, Ruth Linssen, Quality in Crime Prevention, Books on Demand GmbH, Norderstedt 2005, pp. 9-40.

Background

Two imbalances (external and internal) that affect effective crime prevention have been noted by the United Nations.

Concerning the first imbalance, since the 1980s, especially in the developing world, there has been a shortage of basic urban services. In 1987, the World Commission on Environment and Development (*"The Brundtland Commission"*) reported to the United Nations General Assembly that "in the space of one decade, the developing world will have to increase by 65 % its capacity to produce and manage its urban infrastructure, and shelter – merely to maintain present conditions"[5]. In 1997, the Secretary-General assessed that the recommended result be, at best mixed, if not met[6].

Cities in developing countries seem especially to be falling short in social services, because of rapid urban migration (mainly because of this process in developing countries, for the first time ever, in 2008, half of the world's population will live in cities). A prime example is Africa. There, the urban population increased nine-fold between 1950 and 2000, rising from 33 million to 295 million in half a century. In Asia, Latin America and the Caribbean, urban population increased by more than five-fold each, from 232 million to 1.4 billion in Asia and from 70 million to 393 million in Latin American and the Caribbean[7]. Developing a balanced urban counteraction to crime, concomitant with migration, is one of the most important global changes in the years to come.

Secondly, in 2005-2007, the question of providing internally balanced social (read: crime prevention and criminal justice) services returned to the United Nations through the Commission on Crime Prevention and Criminal Justice. In 2005 and 2006, the Commission recommended, and the ECOSOC adopted, two resolutions (2005/22 and 2006/20) in which it first requested the UNODC to pay due attention to crime prevention with a view to achieving a balanced approach between crime prevention and criminal justice responses.

In 2007, the Commission heard statements emphasising that crime issues were linked to the level of inclusion of new arrivals, the ability of cities to provide the services needed and the extent to which those groups trusted and participated in the governing of the city. It was noted that there was a need to improve both the level of safety and the overall quality of life for ur-

---

[5] A/42/427, Report of the World Commission on Environment and Development. Note by the Secretary-General, section II, para. 71.
http://www.are.admin.ch/imperia/md/content/are/nachhaltigeentwicklung/brundtland_bericht.pdf.
[6] E/CN. 17/1997/3, Commission on Sustainable Development, Global change and sustainable development: critical trends, Report of the Secretary-General, paras. 189 and 205.
[7] Ibid.

ban residents and that human security and urban crime prevention were policy matters of high priority in many countries[8].

In conclusion, over the course of twenty years (1987-2007), the United Nations addressed the question of two imbalances: an external imbalance (shortage of basic urban services amid rapid population growth), and an internal imbalance between preventive and justice responses to crime, in the wake of urbanisation.

Addressing the latter imbalance entails solving a practical question: how to respond to urban crime, whether with punitive or/and with social policy? The reflex response is punitive[9], but it does not work.

A case in point is the experience of South Africa and the USA in combating gangs. There, street and prison gangs have a joint street/prison membership. Those imprisoned enjoy a higher status in the prison because of their original affiliation with a street gang. Imprisonment as such, merely changes the status of gang membership which is reactivated after their release[10]. In the absence of other life opportunities, rejoining the street gang is the only choice[11]. In a city habitat, under present conditions of governance, the State can neither satisfy legitimate basic security nor livelihood needs for marginalised youth. This makes room for gangs with their own version of support. This also perpetuates violence, but to a different degree across cities throughout the world[12], probably because of a different policy response to the problem.

The range of the above responses can be graphically described (Figure 1).

---

[8] E/CN. 15/2007/30, Report on the sixteenth session of the Commission on Crime Prevention and Control, chapter II. A., para. 16.

[9] Irwin Waller, Less Law. More Order, Westport, Connecticut–London, Praeger, 2006, p. 1.

[10] Jonny Steinberg, The Number, Johannesburg, Jonathan Ball Publishers 2004.

[11] Why street thugs are getting nastier, The Economist, 24 February 2005, http://www.economist.com/world/na/displayStory.cfm?story_id=3700336.

[12] There are also other reasons than the development of gangs involved in the spread of urban violence and other crime. For example, other violent entrepreneurs (e.g., organised criminals) may emerge who control a certain location and seek to increase their influence over new locations.

Figure 1 Three models to respond to urban crime

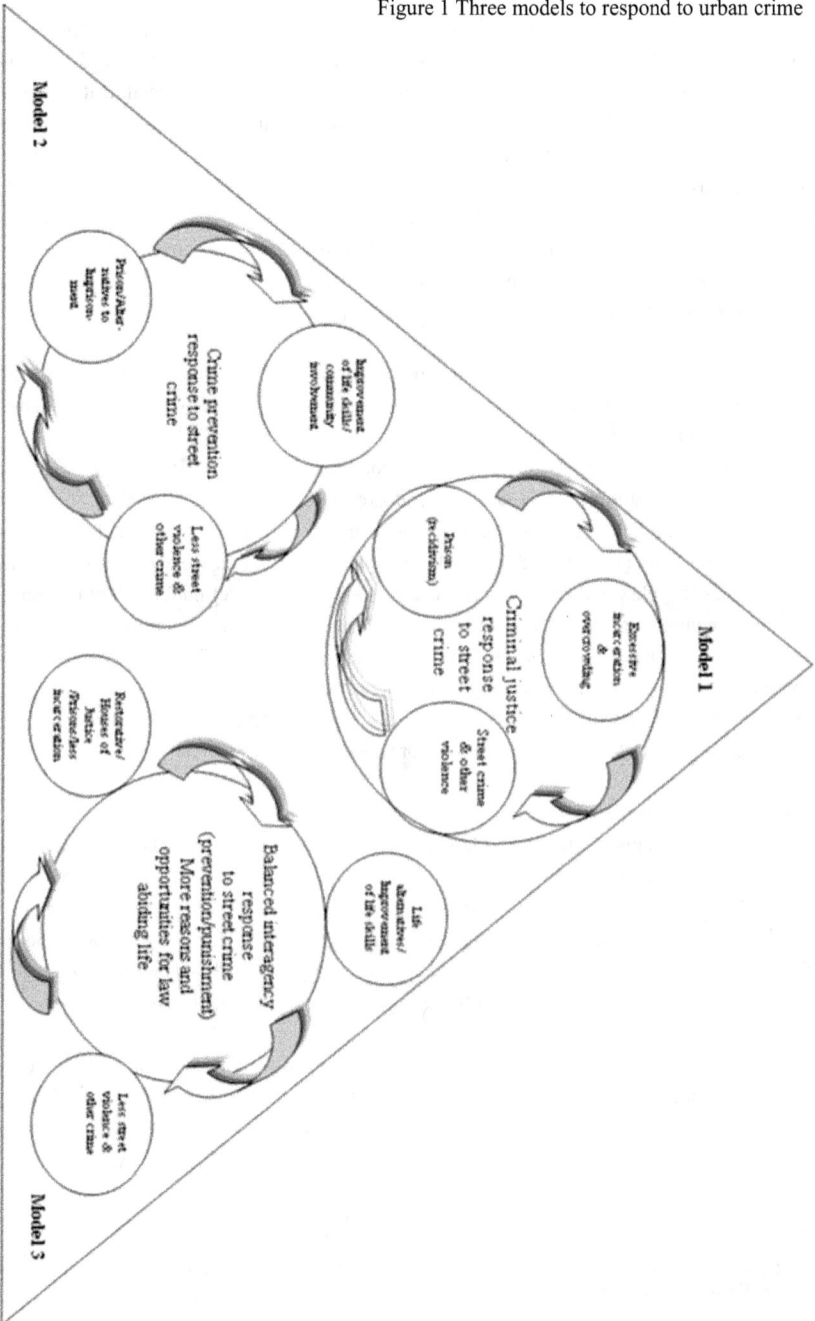

Model 2

Prevent/Alternatives to incarceration

Crime prevention response to street crime

Improvement of life skills/ community involvement

Less street violence & other crime

Model 1

Prison (recidivism)

Criminal justice response to street crime

Excessive incarceration & overcrowding

Street crime & other violence

Restorative/ Houses of Justice/Prisons/less incarceration

Balanced interagency response to street crime (prevention/punishment) More reasons and opportunities for law abiding life

Life alternatives/ Improvement of life skills

Less street violence & other crime

Model 3

There are three models on one graph. Model 1 demonstrates the "criminal justice response" to "youth crime" (in brief). The model shows that street crime is self-perpetuating, enduring (incapacitation rather than rehabilitation) and additionally potentially detrimental, if it results in prison overcrowding. "Get tough" offers no viable solution. Furthermore, model 2, which can be called the "crime prevention response", offers a "soft" approach to youth crime: social and situational crime prevention with alternative life opportunities (sustainable livelihood for street/residence/community groups). Moreover, model 3 is the combination of both earlier models, where community-centered preventive and justice responses (prisons/restorative justice/houses of justice/sustainable livelihood opportunities for growing in culture of lawfulness through education and legitimate entrepreneurship) have been mixed.

The third model seems to be gaining popularity and working. Various research results (structural and delinquents/offender-based), come to similar conclusions. For example, the World Bank study[13] of the impact of crime and violence on the economic development of Brazil emphasises that counteracting the problem is far more than a criminal justice issue. No single intervention, no matter how well designed and executed, will solve the problem. There are multiple entry points likely to pay large dividends in reducing crime and violence. They include prevention programs targeting at-risk youth and gender-based violence, controlling the sale of alcohol, police reform, and integrated municipal (and state) public safety programs. While it is common to argue for either prevention or control responses to crime and violence, the two types of interventions are in fact complementary. A more efficient and professional criminal justice system - and especially police forces with new policing styles - is essential to lower levels of impunity. At the same time, many types of crime and violence are most appropriately and cost-effectively dealt with by prevention activities.

This is also the conclusion from the research in the United States, quoted in support of the above recommendation by the World Bank. That research found that a reduction of between 0.49 and 0.66 violent crimes by juveniles is achieved for each year of delinquent-custody (that is, counting equally one delinquent held for one year and six delinquents held for two months each, for example). Thus, the data suggests tougher enforcement reduces juvenile crime today. But the severity of the juvenile justice system during the last year (before becoming an adult) does not have a statistically significant impact on adult criminal behaviour.

This suggests that the deterrence or incapacitation effect of juvenile punishment is counterbalanced by the "criminal human capital/stigma" effects of being held in custody. Thus, a more punitive juvenile justice system may reduce juvenile crime today, but it will not reduce

---

[13] Report No. 36525, Crime, Violence and Economic Development in Brazil: Elements for Effective Public Policy, World Bank, June 2006.

crime among today's juveniles when they are adults - since being held in custody increases the likelihood of a return to criminality or decreases that of a return to legal activity[14].

Crime prevention works and there have now been numerous other confirmations of this, including most recently reviews and conclusions by eminent international crime prevention experts[15]. They all say: "*Let crime prevention work*".

I. Apply the rule of law: the principle of the rule of law[16]

More than 120 years have passed since a British constitutionalist, A.V. Dicey (1885) made a first theoretical contribution to the development of the principle of the rule of law until its international working definition by the Secretary-General of the United Nations (2004). According to the latter, the rule of law refers to "a principle of governance in which all persons, institutions and entities, public and private, including the State itself, are accountable to laws that are publicly promulgated, equally enforced and independently adjudicated, and which are consistent with international human rights norms and standards. It requires, as well, measures to ensure adherence to the principles of supremacy of law, equality before the law, accountability to the law, fairness in the application of the law, separation of powers, participation in decision-making, legal certainty, avoidance of arbitrariness and procedural and legal transparency" [17].

At the forefront of that concept of the rule of law stands prevention, which is "worth significantly more than a pound of cure", if security needs, the unequal distribution of wealth and social services, the abuse of power and ethnic discrimination are addressed through it [18].

Between 1885 and now, the concept and the practice of the rule of law has been significantly advanced, to the point that sophisticated analytical models by the World Bank suggest that there is now a group of developed countries in the world with a very high level of observing the rule of law (Table 1)[19].

---

[14] Steven D. Levitt, Juvenile Crime and Punishment, Journal of Political Economy, University of Chicago Press, 1998, vol. 106 (6), pp. 1156-1185.

[15] See articles by Anthony Bottoms, Hans-Jürgen Kerner and Irwin Waller in UNAFEI Resource Material Series No. 68, March 2006.

[16] Section 2.3 (c) (vii) and (d) (i) c. of the 1995 ECOSOC Guidelines ("Integrated crime prevention action plan"), section III.12 of the 2002 ECOSOC guidelines ("Basic principles"), and IV C. 25 (d) ("Social development").

[17] S/2004/616, Report of the Secretary-General on the rule of law and transitional justice in conflict and post-conflict societies, para. 6.

[18] Ibid, para. 4

[19] The governance indicators presented here aggregate the views on the quality of governance provided by a large number of enterprise, citizen and expert survey respondents in industrial and developing countries. This data is gathered from a number of survey institutes, think tanks, non-governmental organisations, and international organisations. The rule of law measures the extent to which agents have confidence in, and abide by the

Table 1 Rule of law in selected developed and developing countries by percentile rank (2006)

Developed country	Rank (0-100)	Developing country	Rank (0-100)
AUSTRIA	97.1	BOTSWANA	67.1
CANADA	96.2	BRAZIL	41.4
CZECH REPUBLIC	73.3	DOMINICAN REPUBLIC	39.5
FINLAND	98.1	EL SALVADOR	37.6
FRANCE	89.5	ETHIOPIA	30.0
GERMANY	94.3	GHANA	51.0
GREECE	67.6	GUATEMALA	14.3
ISRAEL	70.0	HAITI	2.4
ITALY	60.0	JAMAICA	33.3
NORWAY	99.0	KENYA	15.7
POLAND	59.0	MEXICO	40.5
PORTUGAL	82.9	NIGERIA	8.1
RUSSIA	19.0	REPUBLIC OF SOUTH KOREA	72.9
SLOVENIA	75.2	RWANDA	34.3
SPAIN	84.8	SOUTH AFRICA	58.6
SWEDEN	96.7	UGANDA	39.0

rules of society, in particular the quality of contract enforcement, the police, and the courts, as well as the likelihood of crime and violence. The percentile rank of a country indicates its position among 1 212 countries/territories in the world covered by the ranking. 0 corresponds to lowest rank and 100 to highest rank. There is no established convention for the designation of "developed" and "developing" country. In the latter category, some countries belong to the group of "least developed". The methodology for collecting the constitutive elements of the rule of law indicator is described in: A Decade in Measuring the Quality of Governance. Governance Matters 2006,Worldwide Governance Indicators, The International Bank for Reconstruction and Development, Washington, D. C., 2006, http://siteresources.worldbank.org/INTWBIGOVANTCOR/Resources/1740479-115040258235 7/2661829-1158008871017/booklet_decade_of_measuring_governance.pdf.

UNITED KINGDOM	93.3	Subsaharan Africa	28.8
UNITED STATES	91.9	Latin America	35.4
Organisation for Economic Cooperation and Development	90.0	Caribbean	65.0

Source: Daniel Kaufmann, Aart Kraay and Massimo Mastruzzi, Governance Matters VI: Governance Indicators for 1996-2006 (July 2007), *World Bank Policy Research Working Paper* No. 4280

Among them is Germany, one of the sponsors of the aforementioned 2002 ECOSOC resolution, with the crime prevention guidelines that stress the importance of applying the rule of law. The table also covers a number of developing countries among which there are notable exceptions showing high level of observance of the rule of law[20]. By and large, however, the difference between developed and developing countries is clear.

Accordingly, in the African countries, estimates suggest that court decisions cover less than 10 per cent of the urban crime (major and minor delinquencies included)[21]. In the slum areas of Africa (eg. Ghana, Kenya, Nigeria, South Africa)[22] and Central America (eg. Guatemala[23]), known for their insecurity, their residents exercise "do-it-yourself" (mob) justice, without legal authority, by lynching or beating the alleged criminals to death, with a tacit approval of the police. The police not only look away, but are reluctant to enter the slum areas. Underpaid, under resourced, often corrupt, the police do not enforce the law consistently with international human rights norms and standards. They do not uphold the supremacy of law, accountability to the law, fairness in the application of the law, avoid arbitrariness and follow procedural and legal transparency. Why, then, do neither the victimised nor the authorities *"Apply the rule of law"*?

Such lawlessness has many reasons. The ECOSOC guidelines addressed some of them in the two subsequent principles.

---

[20] Some other developed and developing countries included in Table 1 have also been included in other sections of this article.

[21] Juma Assiago, Promoting Urban Crime Prevention Strategies in Africa, http://ww2.unhabitat.org/programmes/safercities/documents/Urban_Crime_Prevention.PDF, p. 2.

[22] Is mob justice acceptable ? 13 October 2000, http://news.bbc.co.uk/1/hi/talking_point/debates/african/965299.stm; Jeremy Clark, Kenyan police kill 11 in Nairobi gang crackdown, 7 June 2007, http://www.alertnet.org/thenews/newsdesk/L07639405.htm.

[23] Crime and Development in Central America. Caught in the Crossfire, United Nations Office on Drugs and Crime, Vienna May 2007, http://www.unodc.org/pdf/Central%20America%20Study.pdf , p. 81.

II. Include marginalised people in the legitimate socio-economic activities: the principle of socio-economic inclusion[24]

Marginalisation is one of such reasons for lawlessness. Marginalised communities grow in violence; their members offend and victimise more vulnerable individuals (women, children) who physically and mentally suffer the effects of exclusion.

The source of marginalisation is the retreat of the welfare state, and the emergence of punitive policies toward members of marginalised communities. That retreat made more than 500 million workers additionally available at the supply side of a progressively global labour market[25]. Within that group, which is only partly formally registered as unemployed, there are an estimated 66 million unemployed young people. In 2005, the youth unemployment rate stood at 13.5 per cent (compared to 6.4 per cent for the overall global unemployment rate and 4.5 per cent for the adult unemployment rate). At least 50 of the countries for which data are available have youth unemployment rates of more than 15 per cent[26].

In general, the youth (15-19 years of age) of this decade (2005) are less economically active than that of 1990. Females are less economically active than males, but all are more educated (the school enrolment ratio grew)[27]. In the 15-24 age category (most prone to drugs, crime and sexual exploitation), in the years 1995-2005, unemployment grew by almost 15 %. There are idler, but better educated youths around, on an oversupplied job market riddled with insecurity. Those 300 million unemployed, the "youth bulge" (approximately 25% of the entire youth world population), live below the US $2 per day poverty line[28]. This bulge is disproportionately driven by population growth of developing countries. Every hour in: Istanbul (Turkey) 28 children are born, Mexico City (Mexico) +31, São Paolo (Brazil) and Karachi (Pakistan) +33, in Mumbai (India) +43, and in Lagos (Nigeria) +53. At the same time, in Los Angeles (USA) +20, in Tokyo (Japan) +5, in Seoul (Republic of Korea) +2, while elsewhere there is negative population growth: in London (UK), Milan (Italy) and Madrid (Spain) -3, and in Moscow (Russia) -5[29].

Presently, Sub-Saharan Africa has the highest proportion of youth (10-24 years of age) in the world - 33%, and experiences a very radical drop (1990-2005) of labour market opportunities

---

[24] Section III. 8 of the 2002 ECOSOC guidelines ("Basic principles").

[25] Peter Lock, Crime and violence: Global economic parameters (2006), http://www.libertysecurity.org/article940.html.

[26] Youth Employment World Youth Report, 2003, www.un.org/esa/socdev/unyin/documents/ch02.pdf, p. 4.

[27] See further: U.S. Population Reference Bureau, The World's Youth Population Data Sheet 2006, page 6, http://www.prb.org/pdf06/WorldsYouth2006DataSheet.pdf.

[28] Lock, op. cit.

[29] Ricky Burdett, Urban age project, Urban Age Johannesburg Conference 2006, http://www.urban-age.net/0_downloads/pdf_presentations/Johannesburg/A3_Burdett.pdf .

for youth of 15-19 years of age, especially men. It has also the fastest urbanising rate of all continents. Some 49% of the population lives there on less than US $1 a day (70% in urban slums), and their numbers are expected to double every 15 years on average. Indeed, the estimated percentage of the populations living in slum areas is a very telling single measure of the socio-economic exclusion in most of the developing countries.

The formation of gangs is one of the results of exclusion. Gangs are "organisations of socially excluded"[30]. They are the symptom of the strengthening of sub-cultural identities by men and women who resist marginalisation. Even though there are no comprehensive statistics to document this process, results of fragmentary studies indicate that in several countries in Northern, Central and Latin America, and Africa the emergence of youth "gangs"/"organised armed groups" or other youth criminal associations is a fact of life[31]. And so it is in Asia (eg. India and Pakistan) and Europe (eg. France, Poland, Russia, United Kingdom).

Depending on the definition, there are at least tens of millions of gang members in the world today[32]. Consisting of the deprived, and materially and hedonistically motivated (more educated) youth, gangs offer youth a "home" and facilitate their pursuits. Drugs and crime are among them. Gangs are becoming a new common denominator and threat to urban security across the world.

Against these odds, it is widely argued that providing marginalised people with employment/education or involving youth in sport activities reduces the risk of their conflict with law. And indeed, particularly concerning the youth at risk, there is unequivocal empirical evidence that the better education youths receive, the less they offend, especially when they are later employed[33].

But the matter of imparting such life skills is even more complex than this. While employment is superficially beneficial, as to detract from the criminogenic nature of unemployment, questions exist as to its blanket appeal in the reduction of youth crime; there are conditions of youth employment which may induce criminal behaviour[34]. These factors relate to the meaningfulness of the work. Youth employment may be low skilled and low paid. Where the em-

---

[30] John M. Hagedorn, The Global Impact of Gangs, Journal of Contemporary Criminal Justice, 2005, vol. 21, no. 2, p. 156.

[31] See: Crime and Development in Central America, op. cit., and Neither War nor Peace. Children and Youth in Organized Armed Violence. International Comparisons of Children and Youth in Organized Armed Violence, Viva Rio, Rio de Janeiro 2004, Coalition Against, http://www.coav.org.br.

[32] Hagedorn, op. cit., p. 156.

[33] A total of 80 studies from Europe, North America and various international countries reveal a correlation between crime and unemployment (Lee Ellis and Anthony Walsh, Criminology. A Global Perspective, Boston, Pearson-Longman 2005, p. 194).

[34] Nicolas Williams, Francis T. Cullen, John Paul Wright, Labour market participation and youth crime: the neglect of "working" in delinquency research, Social Pathology, Fall 1996, Vol. 2, No 3, 195.

ployer interest in the youth is merely economic and there is no opportunity for personal growth, where there is no mentoring, where the youth is largely unsupervised and the work is not mentally challenging, the likelihood of criminality can be enhanced, and the inclusion process remains on paper only.

And likewise with education. What matters is not its formality but quality. Again, only such educational curricula which are meaningful and motivated by the implementation of the principle of inclusion into the culture of lawfulness, i.e. a rejection of violent, criminal or abusive cultural norms, can have a higher probability of crime prevention success[35]. However, high rates of geographical mobility impact negatively upon school performance, because it weakens the consensus of values, norms and goals[36]. In conclusion, and despite this challenge: "*Include marginalised people in the legitimate socio-economic activities*".

III. Focus on community: the principle of community-centred action[37]

Mobility also affects community life, and weakens the sense of "belonging" - otherwise a powerful incentive for dealing with its problems. They can be tackled locally and with the insight of the local people. Their insight and support prevents moral deterioration in a community, and its physical degeneration which is a visible symptom ("broken windows") of an increase in crime. Where community integration exists, eg. strong community identity along ethnic or religious lines, residents can use this as a starting point for organising crime prevention activities. Juvenile delinquency, for example, may originate from boredom and a lack of both challenge and recreational facilities for young people in the area. The establishment of such facilities and a dispute resolution mechanism could prevent or settle consequent hostilities between neighbours. Where there are well planned crime prevention strategies with the increasing support of a culture of lawfulness, crime, delinquency and victimisation are reduced. The community is inherently safer, the quality of life enhanced, the load on the criminal justice system is reduced and the cost of crime plummets. Here again the need for a balanced preventive and justice response to crime comes into picture, through various conflict resolution mechanisms ("houses of justice"), noted in the background (Figure 1).

An essential element in focussing on the community is the family. The 2002 ECOSOC guidelines emphasise that violence is an intergenerational issue, transmitted from parents to children who carry them on and demonstrate it in school ("bullying").

---

[35] Mayra Buvinic, Andrew Morisson, Michael Shifter, Violence in Latin America and the Caribbean: A Framework for Action, Technical Study, Sustainable Development Department, International Development Bank, Washington, D.C., 1999.

[36] R. D. Crutchfield, M. R. Geerken, W. R. Gove, Crime rate and social integration, Criminology, vol. 20, no 3 /4, Nov. 1982, pp. 467-478; United Nations World Youth Report 2005, United Nations, New York 2005, p. 138.

[37] Sections 1.1 and 2.3 (b) (ii) and 3 (c) (vi) of the 1995 ECOSOC guidelines ("Local approach to problems" and "Integrated crime prevention action plan") and section III. 8, and IV. 16 of the 2002 ECOSOC guidelines ("Socio-economic development and inclusion", and "Community involvement") .

There are many programmes that aim to provide parents and families with the skills to take better physical and psychological care of children and youth. There is evidence that they are very effective in preventing substance abuse and a range of other problematic behaviour. Studies of the World Health Organisation (WHO) indicate that there is also growing evidence that parenting practices can be powerful risk or protective factors for unhealthy behaviour of children and youth, across cultural settings[38]. However, there is also evidence, again from an extensive review done by the WHO, that family skills programmes and other kinds of family-based interventions are not frequently implemented, especially in low and middle income countries. Main implementation obstacles include the lack of implementation protocols adapted to local culture/situation and the difficulties of involving parents and guardians whose time and energy are already stretched to provide basic sustenance for the family.

There are a growing number of projects, evaluations and meta reviews of the influence of community-centred and family-based urban crime prevention in developing and developed nations, most of which equivocally document the benefits of this approach. What is needed is to develop and test an implementation model (which would include: guidelines, training materials for the parents/children/families) to be used in low and middle income countries, with a "*Focus on community*" and family.

IV. Work on interagency basis: the principle of partnership[39]

Traditionally, crime prevention and control has been the responsibility of the law enforcement, i.e., the police, as well as prosecutorial and correctional entities. But the urbanisation of crime has rearranged the landscape for its counteraction. Law enforcement alone or law enforcement as a centrepiece of local counteraction to crime no longer remains a tenable principle. The principle of partnership among various entities is now the only tenable one.

There are many national examples of such a new partnership approach. Not all worked. What works follows the meticulously reviewed experience of the "whole of government" approach in the United Kingdom[40].

This approach is built on the assumption that because we know the causes of crime are complex and multifaceted, then preventive responses will be more effective if we combine the efforts of all the relevant government agencies (and community and business groups) into a

---

[38] The WHO Child and Adolescent Health and Development Programme (ACH) has been working on this. See, e.g., Growing in confidence. Lessons from eight countries in successful scaling up of adolescent health and development programming, http://www.who.int/child-adolescent health/New_Publications/ADH/WHO_FCH_CAH_02.13.pdf

[39] Section 2. 3 (b) of the 1995 ECOSOC Guidelines ("Integrated crime prevention plan"), and section II.5, III. 7, 9, 17 and 19 of the 2002 ECOSOC Guidelines ("Conceptual frame of reference", and "Basic principles").

[40] By Peter Homel, The whole of government approach to crime prevention, Trends and Issues in Crime and Criminal Justice, No. 287, November 2004, pp. 1-6, author of the motto of the present article.

single coordinated strategy. However, using a detailed analysis of the experience of the British Crime Reduction Programme, it was found that implementing a whole of government approach can present many practical challenges and difficulties that need to be carefully planned for and managed in order that the improved benefits can be seen to outweigh the additional costs.

The conclusions are as follows:

As there are multiple entry points to prevent crime and violence, start with those that have potential for effective bilateral partnerships or joint inter-agency arrangements;

Avoid duplication of efforts (information systems; data requirements, etc.);
Achieve policy goals through problem analysis and assessment of best practice/best value evidence;
Find a way of including crime prevention within a broader social justice framework that will help to develop initiatives regenerating communities;
To this end, transfer economic and political resources to local institutions and residents, thus empowering communities, helping to integrate the marginalised youth, and enabling to tackle key community-level risk factors of crime and delinquency;
Continue towards coherent and effective central management.
In sum, "*Work on interagency-basis*", bottom–up.

V. Make crime prevention a renewable resource: the principle of sustainability and accountability[41]

The full meaning of the above conclusion (and of the other conclusions stemming from the application of principles I-IV) can best be appreciated in the context of the principle of sustainability.

This is because of the aforementioned report of the "*Brundtland Commission*" (1987) through which the United Nations embarked on a ground-breaking mission of facilitating globally sustainable development as development that "meets the needs of the present without compromising the ability of future generations to meet their own needs"[42]. The report highlighted three fundamental components to sustainable development: environmental protection, economic growth and social equity.

---

[41] Sections III. 10 ("Sustainability/accountability"), IV. A. 20 ("Sustainability"), and B. 22 (c) ("Planning interventions").
[42] A/42/427, op. cit., para. 27.

Although that report did not directly deal with crime issues (this was the pre-globalisation era of crime), in the 1990s, the goal of alternative development for the prevention of illicit drug cultivation, and then the goal of crime prevention for sustainable development (ECOSOC resolutions 2002/13 and 2005/22, operative para. 4), both entered the United Nations drugs and crime agenda in their own ways. Making crime prevention work requires managing it successfully for the purpose of sustainable development ("smart growth"[43]).

The 2002 ECOSOC guidelines emphasise three dimensions of sustainability: programmatic, institutional and financial.

Programmatically, the guidelines declare that Governments and other funding bodies should strive to achieve sustainability of demonstrably effective crime prevention programmes and initiatives through, inter alia: (a) encouraging community involvement in sustainability and (b) reviewing resource allocation to establish and maintain an appropriate balance between crime prevention and the criminal justice and other systems, to be more effective in preventing crime and victimisation. Institutionally, the guidelines recommend establishing clear accountability for funding, programming and coordinating crime prevention initiatives. Finally, financially, the guidelines also declare that crime prevention requires adequate resources, including funding for structures and activities, in order to be sustained. There should be clear accountability for implementation and evaluation and for the achievement of planned results.

Behind this rather formalistic concept there is something more lively: the debate over the practical implementation of the concept of crime prevention as a renewable resource developed by the energies of community. How this resource performs, depends on the specific concepts and methods with which it is approached[44]. Surely, the performance should be measurable and accountable (base-line data, safety audits). This functional sense of sustainability is, perhaps, the most essential for successful crime prevention. It has numerous other practical and theoretical implications, including the need to revisit and reinterpret criminological theories, in terms of etiology and prevention of crime, and their field application, in line with the motto *"Make crime prevention a renewable resource"*.

---

[43] Richard H. Schneider, Ted Kitchen, Crime Prevention and the Built Environment, London and New York, Routledge, Taylor and Francis Group 2007, p. 35.

[44] See, e.g., Rachel Armitage, Sustainability versus safety: confusion, conflict and contradiction in designing out crime, (in:) Graham Farrell, Kate J. Bowers, Shane D. Johnson (eds), Imagination for Crime Prevention. Essays in Honour of Ken Pease, Crime Prevention Studies, Vol. 21, Criminal Justice Press, Monsey, NY, USA, Willan Publishing, Cullompton, Devon, UK, 2007, pp. 81-110.

VI. Apply knowledge: the principle of evidence-based practice[45]

Knowledge is not cast in stone. It is the best knowledge we have, at any given time, about crime, based on the best analytical work available and supporting empirical study[46].

Verification of what works in crime prevention is based on various ever updated scientific research methods and protocols. In the developed world, where evidence and not ideology prevails, researchers found that the conclusions of the effectiveness of a programme are stronger the larger the number of people (such as youth at risk) that went through the programme, the more often the programmes have been tested in different locations, and the more the results were evaluated by an independent expert who compared them with those who went through the programme with a similar or identical group of people[47]. The conclusions echo the conclusions from a review twenty years later that had already shown that imprisonment did not work, but that programmes targeted to risk factors that lead to crime might work if given sufficient resources[48]. However, Governments should be the leaders in crime prevention, not only by providing resources and expertise, but also in training, qualifying and certifying all professionals[49].

Particularly valuable practices have been pursued intergovernmentally by the European Union's Crime Prevention Network which employs a peer review process, and by non-governmental entities, like The Campbell Crime and Justice Coordinating Group which pursues systematic crime prevention reviews. These reviews employ scientific and explicit methods to identify, screen, appraise and analyse evaluation studies. This kind of rigorous review produces the most reliable evidence on what the science says about a particular question[50].

In the developing world these conclusions and methods can only be partly pursued. The application of the ECOSOC crime prevention guidelines is still more rights- rather than evidence-based. What is so obvious in Europe, Northern America, Australia, Japan, Republic of Korea and in a few developing countries (*e.g.* Brazil and South Africa), in the other countries is still a postulate which the international donor and research community should address, that is to "*Apply knowledge*".

---

[45] Section B. 2.5 (d) of the 1995 ECOSOC guidelines ("Authorities at all levels") and section IV. B. 21 and 23 of the 2002 ECOSOC guidelines ("Knowledge base", and "Support evaluation").

[46] Per-Olof H. Wikström, Doing without knowing. Common pitfalls in crime prevention, (in:) Farrell et. al., op. cit,. p. 61.

[47] Larry Sherman, quoted in Irwin Waller, Less Law..., op. cit., p. 18.

[48] Ibid.

[49] For crime prevention as an educational subject, see: Kauko Aromaa, Sławomir Redo (eds), For the Rule of Law: Criminal Justice Teaching and Training @cross the World, The European Institute for Crime Prevention and Control, affiliated with the United Nations (HEUNI), The Korean Institute of Criminal Justice Policy (Helsinki – Seoul 2008).

[50] See also: Erich Marks, Anja Meyer, Ruth Linssen, The Beccaria-project, op. cit.

Conclusion

The six United Nations guiding principles to make crime prevention work have not only a substantive but also capacity-building sense. In either case they serve one purpose – to reduce crime in the world in a humane and effective manner. The ECOSOC guidelines, from which they are derived, are promoted and used by the United Nations Office on Drugs and Crime in its own crime prevention project ideas ,and project documents, as the best practice which paves the way to the successful counteraction of crime. Indeed the Secretary-General of the United Nations argued that "prevention is worth significantly more than a pound of cure", and should be seen as the first imperative of justice (S/2004/616).

For the incipient global crime prevention movement this is certainly an encouraging statement for its "smart growth". Consequently, the international crime prevention and criminal justice community now has in its hands a weighty measure that not only challenges the traditional wisdom about what works in counteracting crime, but also which shows the new way worth pursuing.

Margaret Shaw[1]

Why Youth Are Essential Partners in Crime Prevention: An International View

The theme of this year's German Congress on Crime Prevention *Starke Jugend – Starke Zu-kunft* (Strong Youth – Strong Future) is a very apt and important one. In many countries there are now increasing proportions of children and young people, and they often constitute up to half the urban poor. Yet cities and communities responding to crime and insecurity often see young people as 'the problem' or their behaviour as inherently anti-social. There is a long history of interventions which target young offenders already in trouble with the law, and those on the margins of becoming involved in gangs, drugs or minor incivilities. While targeting interventions in this way is an important element in a broader youth prevention strategy, projects which incorporate medium and long term goals, which are inclusive rather than exclusive, and have a strong participatory element would appear to have some important advantages.

This paper reviews the growing focus on *participatory* approaches in crime prevention internationally, and discusses some examples of projects and approaches involving the participation of young people in their planning and development. The paper draws on a range of sources, and aims to provide a brief overview of what we have learned in the recent past about youth and their involvement in urban crime, and the experience gained from many countries on crime prevention. It looks at the principles which should guide our responses to young people and urban crime prevention, established by the UN Guidelines for Crime Prevention (ECOSOC 2002/13), and provides some examples of effective and promising strategies and practice from around the world. Some of these were presented at the Workshop on crime prevention in urban areas and for youth at risk, at the 11th UN Congress on Crime Prevention and Criminal Justice, held in Bangkok in 2005.[2]

What is the problem?

Internationally young people may well be seen as the major problem for cities. In 2007, for the first time, the world's urban population has exceeded that living in rural areas.[3] This rapid urbanisation especially over the past 15 years, has spurred the growth of a number of mega

---

[1] The International Centre for the Prevention of Crime (ICPC), 465 rue St Jean, Suite 803, Montreal, Quebec, H2Y 2R6, Canada. shaw@crime-prevention-intl.org. For more information on ICPC see www.crime-prevention-intl.org.

[2] Shaw & Travers (2007). Strategies and Best Practices in Crime Prevention in particular in relation to Urban Areas and Youth at Risk. Proceedings of the Workshop held at the 11th UN Congress on Crime Prevention & Criminal Justice, Bangkok, Thailand, 18-25th April 2005. Montreal: ICPC.

[3] See UN HABITAT's The State of the World's Cities Report 2006/2007 (2006) and Global Report on Human Settlements 2007 (2007).

cities of over 20 million inhabitants. This includes the growth of informal settlements, in which some 1 billion slum dwellers now live in extremely deprived and difficult conditions. In-migration and immigration have increased the numbers of ethnic and cultural minorities living in cities. There are increasing disparities of income and access to services, housing, education, health and security, and there is long-term poverty and unemployment. Children and young people now represent up to 50% of the population of many cities, especially in less developed countries, and constitute up to half the urban poor.

These children and young people are especially vulnerable to exploitation, crime and victimisation, and growing trans-national organised crime, while trafficking in small arms, drugs and persons, have all facilitated their involvement and exacerbated urban violence.[4] The majority of perpetrators of urban violence are young men aged 15 - 25 years of age, but they are also the majority of victims of that violence. The *World Health Organisation* estimated that some 199,000 youth murders took place globally in 2000, with around 565 children and young people aged 10-29 dying each day of the year. In Brazil, for example, homicides rose from some 13,000 in 1980 to over 50,000 in 2003, and this huge increase is primarily accounted for by the deaths of young, black men, aged 15-25, living in the *favelas*, the poorest areas of big cities. This profile of the victims represents the age, the gender, the colour, and the geography of death, as Silvia Ramos has described it.[5]

In other countries with far lower levels of youth-related homicides, concerns about apparent increases in youth violence seem perennial. A recent increase in deaths of young men in Toronto, associated with guns and drugs, or of youth gun-related crime in England, have been cause for considerable public concern.[6] Yet even uncivil behaviour by young people has become the target of government intervention, whether at the local authority, regional or national level. In England and Wales, for example, the use of the *Anti-Social Behaviour Order* is an illustration of the tendency in that country in particular to 'define deviance up' and resort to deterrent measures to ensure order and civility.[7] Such approaches have been referred to as 'swift, summary and straightforward justice', often appealing to both the public and politicians, but have in fact resulted in the increasing criminalisation of young people involved in minor delinquency.[8]

---

[4] Bevan & Florquin, 2006.

[5] Centre for Studies on Public Security and Citizenship, University of Candido Mendes, Rio de Janiero. See Ramos, 2006a.

[6] For Toronto see, for example, the conference Safe Cities for Youth. A culture of smart choice. March 12-13th 2007 www.toronto.ca/scfy/ . For England & Wales, 'Killings in Manchester and London raise gang feud fears.' The Guardian Weekly 03.08.07 p.17.

[7] Crawford, 2006.

[8] Allen 2006; Newburn, 2007.

The policies which tend to receive most public attention tend to be the short-term or repressive ones, and with increasing use of surveillance and technology. Yet in relation to youth, it is increasingly clear that the escalation in punitive responses to youth violence is unsustainable and ultimately counterproductive. *Mano duro* policies, which have been a primary response to urban youth violence in Latin America and the Caribbean, for example, work against the long term interests of those societies.[9] Nor should young men be viewed as a population to be feared. There has been a tendency, evident in the case of Africa, and Latin America, to view the growing populations of (male) youth in cities as inevitably to be mistrusted and feared, and requiring 'security-driven responses'.[10]

A shift away from repressive approaches, towards more inclusive, participatory and mediating and restorative approaches is evident internationally, nevertheless, and needs to be given much greater public visibility. There are also a number of internationally accepted principles and norms and standards against which to measure the kinds of interventions and initiatives which we develop with young people.

Principles for intervention – the UN Guidelines for Crime Prevention

The UN Guidelines for Crime Prevention adopted in 2002 (ECOSOC 2002/13), provide norms and standards for the development of crime prevention strategies and policies around the world. The Guidelines set out the basic principles for such policies, including the importance of:

- Government leadership
- Socio-economic development and inclusion
- Co-operation and partnerships
- Sustainability and accountability
- Use of a knowledge base
- Human rights and a culture of lawfulness
- Interdependency
- Differentiation

Effective urban crime prevention requires strong leadership from national and local governments; strategic planning based on good analysis of problems and causes; comprehensive strategies which include the whole range of services and institutions affecting peoples daily lives; community-based and problem-solving policing, and strong partnerships between policy makers and providers and civil society. It also requires governments to uphold the human

---

[9] Shaw, 2004, UNODC, 2007
[10] Sommers, 2006.

rights of citizens, and to work against the exclusion of vulnerable groups including the urban poor, women and minorities, and children and young people.

In addition to these principles for effective crime prevention, the 1989 *Convention on the Rights of the Child* (CRC) emphasises not only the right to healthy environments and protection; it also promotes the inclusion and acceptance of children. Article 12, for example, gives them the right to a voice, recognising that they are also citizens who should be able to participate in the ordering of their lives.[11] Articles 13 and 15 recognise their rights to freedom of expression and of association. Nevertheless, while many countries have ratified the *Convention on the Rights of the Child*, few countries currently recognise children and youth as citizens, or ascribe them the status of equal citizenship within their societies. Without involvement in decision-making, children and youth are excluded, and their rights often unrecognised.

In relation to effective policies and programmes with youth, the 2005 UN Congress workshop concluded that effective strategies for preventing and responding to youth offending and victimisation include the following elements:

- Inclusive approaches which reduce youth marginalisation
- Participatory approaches
- Integrated multi-sectoral strategies
- Balanced strategies which include early intervention, social and educational programmes, restorative approaches and crime control
- Targeted and tailored strategies and programmes to meet the needs of specific at-risk groups
- Approaches which respect the rights of children and young people.

Overall, the lessons learned in the North over the past ten years are that carefully balanced and planned strategies, which adhere to those principles, can work to prevent and reduce youth crime. Viewing violence as a public health problem, for example, opens up a much greater range of responses than those restricted to the criminal justice system, and we do have good evidence of effective prevention alternatives.[12] There are now many good examples of effective and successful strategies and programmes which utilise participatory approaches.

However, not all programmes for youth developed in the North American are theoretically or practically the most appropriate models on which to base policy and interventions in other

---

[11] See Bartlett, S. (2002). 'Building better cities with children and youth.' Environment & Urbanization, 14 (2) 3-10.

[12] eg. Welsh, 2005; Shaw, 2005, Guerra, 2005, Allen, 2006.

regions or countries. While the risk, protective and exacerbating factors for involvement in serious youth gang violence, for example, may be similar, not just the scale of the problems, but the complexity of the links with local communities and histories can be very different. The involvement of children and youth in organised armed violence in a number of developing (and developed) countries, often with devastating consequences for their communities and themselves, has been the subject of comparative study in a number of countries.[13] Such groups have been defined as:

'Children and youth employed or otherwise participating in Organised Armed Violence where there are elements of a command structure and power over territory, local population or resources.' *Dowdney 2005 p.15*

Examples have been identified in Colombia, Ecuador, El Salvador, Jamaica, Nigeria, Northern Ireland, the Philippines and South Africa, as well as parts of the United States. They range from groups which do not openly carry arms, but used them for fights with other groups or the police, to groups with are openly armed and patrol their communities. The latter tend to be found in areas without strong state police or security forces, and in some cases, for example, the *Bakassi Boys* in Nigeria, work with local government forces.

The complexity of such groups is well demonstrated by the experience of organised youth gangs in Cape Flats, South Africa.[14] From a series of detailed studies of the origins and characteristics of such groups, often recruiting young boys from the age of 10 or 12, it is evident that they have strong historical links to the state, often play a significant role in the local economy and its social and cultural life, providing support and some income, and in return receive support from those communities. Repressing or removing such groups is neither simple nor effective, given these complex ties, and the huge and growing populations of children and young people who will take their place. It has been argued, therefore, that organised armed violence is a distinct problem which needs to be recognised by cities and national governments, as well as internationally. The segregation of cities, the clear links between social exclusion of marginalised populations and the development and survival of organised armed groups, and their institutionalisation in some countries and cities, all point to the need to invest in other kinds of preventive approaches.[15]

---

[13] Dowdney, 2005; Hagedorn, 2005, 2007.
[14] Leggett 2005; Standing, 2003, 2005, 2006.
[15] Hagedorn, 2005; Standing, 2006.

Inclusive and participatory approaches

Participation is a human rights principle, and as such, it is not a gift or privilege bestowed by adults on children, but the right of every child capable of expressing a view. In other words it is a right for all children – especially the most marginalised and vulnerable in society.[16]

There has been a major movement in many social, health or environmental fields to recognise the value and power of participatory approaches. International organisations such as UNICEF, UNESCO, UNDP and UN-HABITAT, as well as donors and regional organisations such as the World Bank or the Council of Europe, have tried to promote and integrate participatory approaches in their funding and technical assistance. Numerous guides and examples of child and youth participatory approaches and projects now exist.[17]

There has been a movement from the notion of consulting young people, to actual participation in project or initiatives which involve them, or even self-advocacy.[18] Children and young people are increasingly involved in a variety of stages from need assessment to project design, implementation and evaluation as suggested in the list below (Lansdown 2001 : 9)

- Research
- Health monitoring/decisions
- Managing schools etc.
- Evaluating services for younger people
- Peer representation
- Advocacy
- Project design, management
- Campaigning, lobbying
- Analysis & policy development
- Publicity, use of the media
- Conference participation

Some of the most well-known examples are of the inclusion of children and youth through *participatory democracy and budgeting* mechanisms. This approach initially developed in cities in Brazil, provides for a portion of a municipal budget to be allocated to young people, and the establishment of a system of elected youth delegates from all districts, who vote on the use of that budget. A report on the use of participatory budgeting with children and young people in four cities in Brazil, Ecuador and Venezuela, provides clear evidence of their effec-

---

[16] UNICEF Concept Note on Participation. www.unicef.org/india

[17] Eg. Driscoll (2002); UNICEF (2006) Child and Youth Participation Resource Guide.

[18] Lansdown, 2001.

tiveness in building awareness of citizenship, and of the often simple and innovative nature of young people's ideas and solutions to local problems (Cabannes, 2006).

"The concerns articulated by the children...demonstrate their keen awareness of their surroundings and of the problems that affect most people. Their concerns tend to be simple: young people focused on issues basic to their health and well-being. Few unrealistic demands were made. ...They wanted lights in dangerous tunnels, covers for drainage ditches that threatened their safety, window repairs in schools, sports areas that could be completed for a small investment, or a doctor for a local health centre." *Cabannes, 2006 p. 217.*

Thus participatory approaches are applicable with children and young people, both girls and boys, in all kinds of circumstances, including those at risk of crime and victimisation or already involved with the law, as suggested in the table and examples outlined below.

	Young people in cities, schools and communities	*Young people at risk and in conflict with the law*	*Young offenders in custody*	*Young people returning to the community*
Examples of participatory projects and initiatives	Participatory budgeting; youth councils & parliaments	Participatory needs & service assessments, project development, implementation & evaluation	Skills, education and job training, leadership training	Skills and job training, income generation projects, leadership training

In a review of violence prevention in Latin American countries, Moser & McIwaine (2005) recommend an *integrated framework for intervention* which combines analysis of the local context and an asset-based analysis of the causes, costs and consequences of violence.[19]

Such an integrated framework of intervention has been put in place in City of Toronto, Canada, in response to the serious increase in youth gun-related violence in recent years. The *Community Safety Plan* established in 2004, is multi-sectoral, targeted, and focuses on youth engagement and cultural competence.[20] It has four key priorities: strong neighbourhoods, youth opportunities, youth justice and community crisis response. It focuses on 13 priority neighbourhoods where most of the incidents have occurred, works to strengthen neighbourhood supports, and works in partnerships linking the government, local communities and the

---

[19] They discuss seven 'ideal' policy approaches each impacting different categories of urban violence: criminal justice; public health, conflict transformation (eg. through peace building), human rights, citizen security, crime prevention through environmental design, social capital/community driven development.
[20] www.toronto.ca/community_safety

private sector. There is a strong emphasis on providing opportunities for young people in the targeted neighbourhoods, through education and apprenticeship programmes, recreation and cultural involvement, and building on youth participation and engagement. The City of Montreal has similarly established an integrated plan of action, *Villes-gangs de rue*, which combines the work of local service providers, the police and researchers, and works with street gangs in the five city areas most affected by their activities.[21]

In Tasmania, Australia, the *Chance on Main* project targets 14-19 year-olds at serious risk of crime, dropping out of school or training, or becoming homeless and disconnected from their families. It was developed after extensive local consultation which included the young people themselves. The programme uses mentoring by high profile community and sporting personalities, intensive individual support and counselling, family support and hands-on activity programs on and off site, (for example, metal work and computer training).[22] The young people involved are often seen as 'difficult' by mainstream service providers, and the source of concern for police, education and health personnel. The need for an early intervention program for this target group was identified from extensive consultation over the past five years involving all relevant service providers, surveys of the Glenorchy community, but also in-depth consultation with young people. The project activities are developed with the full participation of the young people taking part in the programme.

Elsewhere, in countries with far higher levels of youth-related violence and victimisation, a number of impressive participatory projects can be found. In Brazil, for example, *Luta Pela Paz (Fight for Peace)*, has been developed since 2001 as a partnership project in Rio de Janiero Brazil, by the organisation Viva Rio.[23] It began in a *favela* with serious problems of poverty, marginalisation and armed gangs. The project is open to all young people in area (including young women), and offers a combination of sports (boxing), citizenship, education, work and leadership skills training to provide alternatives to youth gangs and drugs. Based on the experience of working with young people at risk of, or involved in, organised armed violence in Brazil, Dowdney (2005) suggests that it is important to develop low-level projects to build the resistance of children and youth, while longer-term work to reduce the risk factors is undertaken. The value and impact of involving young people directly in the development of youth gang reduction strategies has been underlined by this and other studies.[24] A more recent project developed by Viva Rio which also demonstrates an inclusive and participatory approach is *Viva Favela*, an IT programme which focuses on 'the social and digital inclusion' of children and youth in poor and high crime neighbourhoods.[25]

---

[21] Chamandy, 2006.

[22] Glenorchy City Council, Tasmania. See Australian Institute of Criminology Newsletter No. 28 March 2007.

[23] See Marianna Olinger in Shaw & Travers 2007; and Dowdney, 2005.

[24] eg. Winton, 2004 on the views of youth in Guatemala, UN-HABITAT, 2004.

[25] www.stockholmchallenge.se

Another example of strategic and participatory youth violence prevention is the *Gun Free Towns* project supported by UNDP in two cities in El Salvador (San Martin & Ilopango). The project uses a combination of approaches. They include public education against guns, often involving youth in developing media and other campaigns, gun confiscation and restrictions on gun use, and cultural events in 'high-risk' public spaces to help to reclaim them. Since June 2005, a 41% drop in homicides, a 29% reduction in gun-related crimes, and a reduction in the overall crime rate have been reported. The outcomes demonstrate that political will, careful diagnosis, (including in this case of gun incidence and locations); training of national police and city staff to improve inspection and monitoring, as well as good local community management and participatory approaches with young people, can be very effective.[26]

The *Open School Programme (Escola Aberta)* in Pernumbuco, Brazil provides a further example. Mapping violence in Brazil, youth homicides were found to double over weekends compared with weekdays. The project began in 2002 in the State of Pernumbuco, with the support of UNESCO and other organisations. It involves the opening of schools at weekends to provide cultural and educational opportunities for young people. Parents are also invited. The pilot programme was found to reduce youth crimes around Recife by 30%, and the programme has now been extended and consolidated into public policy and adopted in six other major cities in Brazil.[27]

Fica Vivo (Stay Alive) is a youth programme developed in Belo Horizonte, Brazil.[28] From 1997 to 2001, there was a 100% increase in the number of homicides, with 3256 violent deaths between 1998 and 2002. They were primarily young males under the age of 24, in the most disadvantaged *favelas*. The programme was developed in 2002, by the Study Centre on Crime and Public Safety (CRISP) at the Federal University at Minas Gerais (UFMG) and implemented in partnership with the City, municipal, federal and military police, the public prosecutor's office, business organisations, NGO's and local communities.

The 'Stay Alive' Programme uses a problem-oriented approach including scanning, crime mapping, analysis and assessment of priorities, and has implemented a series of projects targeting youth in these areas. The projects include social support, educational, leisure and sports, workshops on issues affecting youth, including violence, drugs, sexual transmitted diseases, sports, arts performance and computers. Job training has been provided for more than 3000 young people. Thirty months after the implementation of the project, there has been an overall decrease in violent crimes, especially homicides and attempted homicides in the targeted areas. This included a 47% decrease in homicides, a 65% decrease in attempted homicide, and a 46% decrease in bakery robberies in one of the slum areas. This was over a

---

[26] www.comunidadesegura.org
[27] www.comunidadesegura.org
[28] Beato, 2004; Shaw & Travers, 2005.

period when there was an 11% increase in violent crime in the non-violent areas of the city. The success of the programme has been attributed mainly to the use of an integrated approach, and to the involvement and participation of community members. This has stimulated the State and Federal government to support the expansion of the 'Stay Alive' Programme to four other clusters of violent slums in the metropolitan area of Belo Horizonte.

Finally, an outstanding example of a strong *youth-initiated* and *youth-led* project which forms part of the 'Stay Alive' programme, is that developed by the hip-hop AfroReggae Cultural Group from Rio de Janeiro. The cultural group was founded in 1993 in the Vigario Geral *favela*, a place very familiar with racism and violence, including that by the police, who had killed 21 residents that year.[29] In 2002 they decide to develop a project *with the police*, to bridge the gap between police and youth through dialogue, music and culture. While it was not possible to develop the project with the Rio police, they were invited to do so by the State Police and Secretariat of Social Defence of the State of Minas Gerais. *The Youth and the Police* project was piloted in 2004 in the city of Belo Horizonte, and trains police in percussion, graffiti art, street basketball, street dancing and theatre.[30] Since 2006, a permanent group of police work for two weeks every month with young people in the slums, and give joint performances in schools, in public, and in police premises. A major and significant aspect of the project is that the main objective is not to change young people and steer them away from crime, as most youth crime prevention projects do, but to *change the relationships* between the police and young people. On both sides there have been considerable changes in how they view each other.

The project is being monitored and evaluated, but preliminary results reported by Silvia Ramos (2006b) suggest 'strong positive impact on changing the image of the police, both among young slum-dwellers who have direct contact with policemen, and the population at large, when policemen appear in cultural activities in the media.' The impact among the police services themselves is more mixed, especially among those not directly involved in the project, although a high percentage of police in the State see such cultural activities as encouraging greater integration between the police and communities.

Mediating conflicts and strengthening capacities

Other inclusive approaches include the recruitment and training of young people as social mediation agents. Examples can be found in France, Belgium, the Netherlands, Tanzania, and South Africa among other countries.[31] In France, for example, social mediation began around 1989, using volunteers to help solve conflicts occurring at schools in high-risk neighbour-

---

[29] Ramos, 2006b.

[30] Ibid.

[31] See Gray, 2006, Community Safety Workers: An exploratory study of some emerging crime prevention occupations.

hoods. These areas often lacked social cohesion, and local authorities did not always respond to problems. In 1990, public transport companies began using mediation approaches to counter perceived insecurity and incivilities, and a number of youth employment programmes followed suit, to improve relations and resolve conflicts with the help of an impartial third party. By 1997, this mode of intervention was included within the *Contrats locaux de sécurité* to improve conditions in public places, and these mediation techniques are now widely used by local communities, businesses, and public housing and public transport to promote better living conditions among and for citizens.

Many mediation agent positions were created in 1997, as a result of the *emploi jeunes* (youth employment) initiative. This was part of a programme to generate employment in cities, and under a 5-year contract they received 50% of funding from the State. The position of *Adjoints de sécurité* (police auxiliaries) was also created under the youth employment initiative to develop community policing. By the year 2000, there were nearly 20,000 such jobs, providing mediation as well as other services. Many municipalities continued the programme by integrating these services when state funding was cut in 2003.

In South Africa, young people have been recruited as *Community Peace Workers* in a project developed by the German Technical Cooperation (GTZ) and the Department for Safety and Security. The programme's major goals are to prevent crime and support youth development in low-income areas. The project aims to provide young people with the skills to identify and mediate conflict situations in their community. The project was initiated in Nyanga, Western Cape province in 1997, and expanded to Soshanguve in 1999 and Khayelitsha in 2004. The recruits perform volunteer community service for one year, while acquiring experience that may lead to gainful employment. After initial training, half of their day is dedicated to foot patrols, while the other is spent in training sessions where they are given further instruction as conflict mediators and leaders. GTZ gives personal, technical and some financial support for training and operations. This includes the supply of transport and food parcels during duty and training to all workers.

Investing in youth for now and the future

This paper has looked at the principles which should underlie interventions and projects with young people, and guide the development of crime prevention at all levels of government. This includes the importance of undertaking a forward-looking and strategic-planning approach to building strong youth and a strong future for them. These principles and approaches form part of the UN Guidelines for crime prevention, among other norms and standards.

The paper has also explored the expanding range of inclusive and participatory approaches which are being used in many fields, including in relation to crime prevention with young people. Some examples of the use of mediation and capacity-building have also been touched on. The majority of examples discussed in this paper have been drawn from countries outside the European sphere, and often from those with far greater everyday experiences of violent crime and youth exploitation and victimisation. This underlines the fact that youth are not made strong by repression, but by building relationships and investing in them with long-term plans for their immediate, medium and long-term future.

One absence from much of the discussion in this paper relates to girls and young women. While the majority of actual perpetrators and victims of youth crime, including violence, are young males, they do not exist in an un-gendered landscape. Nor are young women unaffected by the crime and violence in which young men are involved. Young women also form a major part of the traffic in human persons. Much work remains to be accomplished in terms of the participation and inclusion of young women in employment and skills training, in community decision-making, in terms of gender relations and relationships, and to prevent the violence which young women are themselves subjected to in personal or public settings.

Reviewing the critical situation of young people in Rwanda, ten years or more after the genocide and post-genocide period, Sommers also notes the absence of attention to young women in many youth prevention polices and programmes. In relation to young men he has argued:

The answer to the youth challenge is not to further marginalise or paint male youth as fearsome security threats. That can only inspire increased alienation and a sense of being cornered. It is, in fact, quite the opposite: unemployed, undereducated young men require positive engagement and appropriate empowerment, and participatory financial and program support. Doing so, promises to allow the array of assets that youth offer - namely their energy, enthusiasm, creativity, resourcefulness, and adaptability - to flourish.'[32]

Bibliography

Allen, Rob. 2006. *From punishment to problem-solving - A new approach to children in trouble.* Centre for Crime and Justice Studies, King's College. London: Centre for Crime and Justice Studies www.kcl.ac.uk/ccjs

Beato, Claudio, C 2005. *Case Study 'Fico Vivo' Homicide Control Project in Belo Horizonte.* The International Bank for Reconstruction & Development /The World Bank, Washington DC.

Bevan, James & Florquin, Nicolas (2006). 'Few options but the gun: Angry young men.' In *Annual Report of the Small Arms Survey 2006: Unfinished Business.* Geneva: Small Arms Survey. www.smallarmssurvey.org

Cabannes, Y. (2006). 'Children and young people build participatory democracy in Latin American cities.' *Environment and Urbanization,* 18 (1) 195-218.

Crawford, Adam. (2006). "Fixing Broken Promises?': Neighbourhood Wardens and Social Capital.' *Urban Studies,* 43 (5/6) pp. 957-976.

---

[32] Sommers, 2006 p. 14.

Dowdney, Luke, (2005). *Neither War not Peace: International Comparisons of Children and Youth in Organized Armed Violence.* Rio de Janiero, Brazil: Viva Rio and COAV.

Driscoll, David. (2002). *Creating Better Cities with Children and Youth: A manual for participation.* UNESCO in collaboration with members of the Growing Up in Cities Project. London: Earthscan

Gray, Sharon. (2006). *Community Safety Workers: An exploratory study of some emerging crime prevention occupations.* Montreal: ICPC.

Guerra, N. (2005). *Youth Crime Prevention.* Community Based Crime and Violence Prevention ion Latin America and the Caribbean. International Bank for Reconstruction and Development. Washington, DC: World Bank.

Lansdown, G. (2001). *Promoting Children's Participation in Democratic Decision-Making.* Florence: UNICEF Innocenti Research Centre.

Leggett, Ted. (2005). 'Terugskiet: Growing up on the street corners of Manenburg, South Africa.' Institute for Security Studies for COAV.

Moser, Caroline O. N. & McIlwaine, Cathy (2006). 'Latin American urban violence as a development concern: Towards a framework for violence reduction.' *World development 34 (1) 89-112*

Newburn, Tim. (2007). 'Tough on Crime.' In Tonry, M. (Ed.) 'Crime, Punishment and Politics in Comparative Perspective'. *Crime and Justice,* Vol. 36. Chicago: University of Chicago Press.

Ramos, Silvia. (2006a). 'Juventude e Violencia'. Presentation at the *Seminario de Prevencao a Violencia e a Criminalidade,* Belo Horizonte, Minas Gerais, Brazil 9-10th November 2006.

Ramos, Silvia. (2006b). 'Youth and the Police'. *Boletim seguranca e cidadania.* Centre for Studies on Public Security and Citizenship. Rio de Janiero: CESeC University of Candido Mendes,.

Shaw, Margaret (2006). *Youth and Gun Violence: The Outstanding Case for Prevention.* Montreal: International Centre for the Prevention of Crime.

Shaw, Margaret & Travers, Kathryn. (2007). *Strategies and Best Practices in Crime Prevention in particular in relation to Urban Areas and Youth at Risk. Proceedings of the Workshop held at the 11th UN Congress on Crime Prevention & Criminal Justice, Bangkok, Thailand, 18-25th April 2005.* Montreal: ICPC.

Shaw, Margaret & Travers, Kathryn. (Eds.) (2005). *Urban Crime and Youth at Risk: Compendium of Promising Strategies and Programme.* Montreal: International Centre for the Prevention of Crime. www.crime-prevention-intl.org

Sommers, Marc. (2006). 'Fearing Africa's Young Men: The case of Rwanda.' *Social Development Papers Conflict Prevention & Reconstruction* No. 32. January. Washington DC: The World Bank.

Standing, André. (2003). 'The social contradictions of organized crime on the Cape Flats.' *ISS Paper 74.* Pretoria: Institute for Security Studies.

Standing, André. (2005). 'The threat of gangs and anti-gang policy.' *ISS Paper 116.* Pretoria: Institute for Security Studies.

Standing, André. (2006). *Organized Crime. A Study from the Cape Flats.* Pretoria: Institute for Security Studies.

UN-HABITAT (2004). *Youth, Children and Urban Governance.* Policy Dialogue Series No. 2. Nairobi: UN HABITAT Global Campaign on Urban Governance.

UN-HABITAT (2006). *The State of the World's Cities 2006/2007.* Earthscan Publications. Nairobi: UN-HABITAT.

UN-HABITAT (2007). *Global Report on Human Settlements 2007.* Earthscan Publications. Nairobi: UN-HABITAT.

UNICEF (2006). *Child and Youth Participation Resource Guide.* East Asia & Pacific Regional Office. Bangkok: UNICEF.

UNODC (2007). *Crime and Development in Central America. Caught in the Crossfire.* Vienna: UNODC.

WHO (World Health Organization). (2002). *World Report on Violence and Health.* Geneva: WHO.

Winton, Ailsa (2004). 'Young people's views on how to tackle gang violence in 'post conflict' Guatemala.' *Environment and Urbanization,* 16 (2) 83-99.

Elizabeth Johnston

The multiple Challenges of Youth facing Violence

Youth, as victims and as offenders, are central to the preoccupations of the European local elected officials. This is why the European Forum for Urban Safety, a non-governmental organisation which brings together some 300 local authorities around issues of crime prevention and urban safety particularly welcomed the opportunity to share with you today some thoughts stemming from cities' experiences as well as the recommendations issued at the Zaragoza Conference.

Challenges

a) Definitions and measures

The first challenge for local actors is that of defining youth. Defining "youth" is neither an easy task nor a purely theoretical one. It is a definition that changes according to the individual's situation (perpetrator or victim, both or neither).

Children in the United Nations' definition are all youth under 18 years of age. Legal majority in Europe is set at 18 years. In many of our European countries however, the age of penal responsibility is 16 years old, in some 14... Penal and civil sanctions change according to the age of the delinquent, which shows how important and yet arbitrary the notion of youth is.
This is a good example of huge discrepancies between our legal systems which makes the establishment of a coherent European policy in the field of juvenile justice all the more difficult. However, one basic trend to be noted is that the ages of penal responsibilities are regularly lowered.

Indeed, it is felt by public opinion, and relayed by politicians, that "offenders are getting younger and younger" and "young offenders are getting more and more violent".

Statistical studies do not corroborate an aggravation of the situation. Studies from the mid 1980s show that petty crime starts at pre-adolescence (around 10 years old), accelerates with adolescence to reach a peak at age 15-16, stagnates, and then decreases during the twenties and thirties. (Farrington, 1986 ; LeBlanc, 1995)

To come back to the definition of youth, I would like to underscore a paradox, well-known by youth workers especially in deprived neighbourhoods.
Young people are increasingly being treated by the criminal justice systems like adults, with tougher sanctions, including adult-like prisons...

However they also enter adulthood later and later. The difficulty of entering the job market and obtaining a stable job, decent housing, the difficulty of starting a family means that these young people are not allowed an "adult" status. While this is a widespread phenomenon in

Europe, this is especially salient in the poorest and most marginalized communities. Poorly educated, social and/or ethnic minorities (who also have to face discrimination in the hiring process and on the housing market.) face even greater challenges entering adulthood.

This is why social and economic integration programs implemented at a local level are instrumental in a wider prevention strategy. A juvenile crime prevention and reduction strategy would fail, however brilliant it may be, if there are no initiatives and investments in providing jobs, housing, health services to young adults.

Has youth violence increased?

One question that has come up since the beginning of this conference is whether youth is more violent and delinquent today than in the past.

While I would not risk myself to provide a single answer, one element I would like to add to the many explanations developed is that a certain rise in violence may be inherent to modern society with its increasing focus on consumers' goods. The importance of cars, motorbikes but also cell phones, Ipods, brand clothes for young people make them great consumers but also increasingly thieves when they cannot afford to buy themselves these goods.

Studies show parallel curves of increases in thefts and increases in unemployment of youth under 25 years old (Lagrange, 2001). The frustration process born out of the coexistence of a consumers' society with mass unemployment mean that this youth violence is not a recent phenomenon that a stricter response could eradicate but a structural consequence of our modern society.

Furthermore, it must be noted that youth violence is particularly visible. Anti social behaviour which is often carried out by youth as well as rebellious acts – against representatives of authorities like schools, the police… - are extremely visible to the general public and often spectacular. This is in opposition to categories of crime like family violence that are more hidden but far more prevalent. Or to white collar crime which has much more economic impact than petty theft but far less everyday visibility. Its great visibility seems to make youth violence particularly difficult to tolerate in our communities.

b) Accepting the complexity of youth violence

Youths generate violence, but are also the victims of violence, violence inflicted by the adult world, by their peers and also by themselves.

This is why there is no single, unilateral solution that will succeed in resolving such complex issues as what commonly is labelled "youth violence".

First of all, is it necessary to remind ourselves that disobedience, identity crisis, at-risk behaviors, even reactive violence to the adult world, are an integral part of adolescence?

Furthermore, it is well established that those children who have been precociously exposed to physical or psychological violence within their family and their environment, will be more inclined to use physical and verbal violence to express themselves.

It would therefore be counterproductive to youth's development to try to suppress all conflicts.

c) Sharing the benefits of European integration

Ensuring that at-risk categories of youth benefit from Europe's development as much as all other categories of the population is a important objective, although it may not seem immediately essential.

Whilst European integration greatly benefits youth who study, travel and live abroad, its benefits has not always reached young people who have trouble leaving even their neighbourhoods. Decision makers must use financial and legal instruments made available at a European level and lobby at a European level so that at-risk categories of youth benefit from Europe as much as all other categories of the population. Only such equal access can avoid the creation of a dual European society.

Strategies developed by policy-makers

Including youth – in the decision-making process
How do interests of youth - which may be specific - co-exist with that of the wider community?

Encouraging participation through youth organisations, youth parliaments and city councils is one method many local authorities have developed in order to better understand young people's needs, to let them share responsibilities in the planning and implementation of programs that will directly concern them. Among others, this is an important process in that it enables to gradually involve adolescents into the adult-world of decision-making, and to position them as actors and not consumers of services.

There are many examples of participatory practices that work well, in schools, community centers, sport organisations throughout European cities. Some communities are even trying to engage with the most marginal and hard to reach groups of youth, represented by street gangs.

The phenomenon of gangs exists everywhere, in the countries of the North as well as the South, in both urban and rural areas. A source of insecurity and an object of speculation, a lot of misapprehension often surrounds this phenomenon; media hype, rumour and perceived ideas all interfere with knowledge. Although gangs have a lot in common, they nevertheless have different forms and characteristics. One thing that all youths in gangs tend to have in common is their difficult or even conflicting relationships with their family, school or social environment. The gang represents a second family, a refuge from a society in which youths feel excluded. The reason for feeling or for effectively being excluded, the ways of reacting to this exclusion, involvement in crime, the links with criminal groups, these are all elements which characterize gangs.

The city of Barcelona has an important number of youth gangs, sometimes created locally, others imported from Central and Latin America. They have become increasingly violent and policing strategies to reduce their impact have failed. The city has decided to establish a constructive dialogue with these gangs or at least those that are willing. The city recognizes the gang as an area of socialisation, as a group to be acknowledged and engages with gang members to design violence reduction strategies. This seems to be a promising practice in so far as it no longer antagonizes youth who are solely looking for a "second family" in gangs, but instead provides them with other actors to work with and with constructive alternatives.

Acting in the child's best interest is an obligation we have given ourselves as nations when signing the European and UN charter on Children's rights.

In most cases, it is relatively easy to understand what is meant by the Child's best interest and how one can act to ensure it.

However, acting in the child's best interest is also major challenge for our policy makers- throughout European cities - when that interest seems to contradict other interests. The most evident example is that of unaccompanied minors.

The arrival in Europe of isolated underage children is a phenomenon which has greatly increased on recent years. These children come mainly from countries affected by war, countries with a critical political, social and economic situation which often forces them into emigration. These are children in an extremely dangerous situation exposed to the risk of exclusion, and without any guardian protection of their rights.

They are also the first preys of high level or low level criminal networks. Without any resources, they rapidly engage in criminal activities, putting themselves and others in danger. They constitute for cities in which they arrive both a child protection issue and a public safety issue.

The current debates focus on the determination of the relevant administration to respond to the problem and on the distribution of responsibilities between the various actors and administrative levels. Solutions to the problem are mainly national or even departmental; no European solution has been conceived yet. European territorial communities need to participate actively in building cooperation to overcome national juridical obstacles and to put the protection of minors first.

But mostly, politicians must have the courage of placing the child's best interest above the local community's fear and prevalent negative feelings towards illegal immigrants. In that, protecting these children from violence (from the violence they would endure and the violence they may generate) is a new challenge for European policymakers at all levels of governance.

Partnerships

Youth violence is a complex, multi-faceted issue that requires multi-agency integrated approaches. It requires that all adults in a community get involved according to the youth's needs, and situations. Today, the adage "it takes a whole village to raise a child" translates into partnerships set up locally involving a wide range of actors. In France, for instance, to tackle troubles faced in school, Teams for Educational success (" équipe de réussite educative") including psychologists, teachers, youth workers, city prevention coordinator have been set up. They work in a coordinated fashion, around a shared strategy, centered on individual at-risk cases, to develop appropriate responses to youth at risk of dropping out or of being expelled.

As in many such fundamental domains, the local authority plays a key role in coordinating agencies and non-governmental organisations. For instance, the City of Budapest provides technical and financial support to a successful Safe Schools project, led by a NGO. This project organises the mentoring of at-risk youth in primary schools by university students.

Local "European strategies"

City to city cooperation, within networks such as the European Forum for Urban Safety or through partnerships with youth-led organisations, can bridge the existing gap between the reality of European integration and the most marginalized communities in our cities. EU funded programmes can be used to finance language or vocational training, which will enable young people to travel abroad and exchange with counterparts, widening professional but also personal horizons. These educational and social programs, implemented with a European dimension, should constitute the cornerstone of prevention strategies at the local level.

Recommendations

The European Forum's mayors, representatives of local and regional authorities, having met in Zaragoza in November 2006 for three days of capitalisation and prospective work, issued recommendations on the themes that they have considered essential. Youth facing violence is amongst them.

Recommendations from the Zaragoza Manifesto

Young people must occupy a central place in our local policies. They must not be considered a danger nor designated as scapegoats for insecurity, especially as they are the first victims of violence in all its forms: suicide, abuse, road violence, precariousness and absence of prospects. They are also subjected to more muted violence, sometimes resulting from our institutions (school, police, social services...). These various types of violence hinder their development, their capacities for learning and proper insertion into society, which can generate new violence. In order to avoid this spiral, prevention must be as comprehensive as possible.

Responses must at once:
Take all aspects of the life of the child and adolescent into account: emotional, psychological, academic and familial, as well as legal status.
Develop the dialogue and contact between generations,
Be based on the participation of young people themselves and the mobilisation of their life instinct,

Be viewed as long term and aim at lasting solutions. The effectiveness of the responses depends more on the quality of dialogue and coherence than on the increase in the number of police, judicial, social or academic measures. If the local echelon of cities allows for stable, community, reactive and multidisciplinary policies, a trans-national approach is also indispensable in face of the growth of migrations and trafficking, and must consider the child as a minor to be protected and the foreign child as holder of a right benefiting from this protection.

Detlef Otto Bönke and Tobias Plate

Crime Prevention Activities from the Perspective of the German Presidency of the European Union[1]

The catalogue of this Congress says: "The presentation will give an overview of the major activities in the field of crime prevention during the German Presidency of the EU. It will provide information about events, conferences and developments in European and other international bodies, especially the European Crime Prevention Network (EUCPN)".

Just three years ago, at the **9th Congress in Stuttgart**, there was the opportunity of giving a presentation about the EUCPN, its structure and work. At that time the EUCPN was undergoing a serious crisis. Lack of secretarial and financial resources, lack of visibility and substantial output were the main deficits. The EUCPN underwent an effective reform process in the meantime, which was initiated by the Member States. Below, we will elucidate the reform process and the activities of the EUCPN. Most of all we seek to find out whether the EUCPN is consolidated now, and if it is a model for the future. First however, we will exchange some information about several other activities in the field of crime prevention during the past 5 months and 19 days.

One cornerstone of international crime prevention activities is of course the Crime Commission of the United Nations Office on Drugs and Crime (short: UNODC), which has 40 Member States, one of which is Germany. This year's session of the Commission was shorter than in the past and lasted only one week. But nevertheless, 18 resolutions were discussed and adopted.

I. 16th Session of the UN Commission on Crime Prevention and Criminal Justice in Vienna, 23-27 April 2007

Beneath is a short overview of the outcome of the last session of the UN Commission on Crime Prevention and Criminal Justice in Vienna:

- The **main topics** in the thematic debate were:

    - Crime prevention activities in the field of **urban crime**

    - Crime prevention responses to the sexual **exploitation of children**

---

[1] For questions please contact: Boenke-de@bmj.bund.de or tobias.plate@bmi.bund.de

Concerning the _resolutions,_ the main issues were

-       The UN Global Initiative to fight **human trafficking** planned by the UNODC and the way MS could influence this initiative.

-       The role of the UNODC in the field of combating **terrorism.**

-       UN principles in crime prevention and criminal justice (**"standards and norms"**) and the utility of further **questionnaires in this field. UNODC formulates and promotes internationally-recognised principles in areas like the protection of victims, alternatives to imprisonment, and the treatment of prisoners. Many countries have relied on these standards while reforming their national law. The Crime Commission is currently evaluating the use of Standards and Norms.**

The EU was able to support **several resolutions** and is increasingly united at the meetings of the Crime Commission. The statements covering the main topics are now prepared, coordinated, and read out by the EU Presidency, which does not preclude Member States from giving their own presentations (but this is becoming less common).

The plans of the Commission for the **future** are as follows:

-       The **topics of the thematic debates** of the following sessions will be **"violence against women"** for 2008 and **"economic fraud and identity-related crime"** or **"penal reform and the reduction of prison overcrowding"** for 2009.
The **12**[th] **UN Crime Congress** will take place in **2010** in Brazil or in Qatar. The agenda and the themes must still be discussed.

II. Activities in the European Union

During the EU Presidency major efforts were undertaken to improve international **judicial cooperation** in criminal matters such as the **EU-wide networking of criminal records**. Agreement was reached by the EU Ministers of Justice to improve the exchange of information on criminal matters. There will be no new centralised European register, but the Framework Decision obliges Member States to inform home states of convictions of their nationals. Another example is the general agreement reached by the Ministers of Justice on cross-border cooperation concerning sentences of probation and alternative sanctions (community service work, social training, and restorative justice).

The relevance of crime prevention in different areas of crime was underlined during the German Presidency. But there was a clear focus on the protection of children and juveniles, especially on child-related offences via the Internet or the so-called new techniques.

The three major activities in this field:

1."European Forum on the Rights of the Child"

The forum, which will meet at regular intervals in future, was held in Berlin with opening statements from Vice President Frattini and Justice Minister Zypries. The launch of the forum was attended by more than 200 experts from different EU institutions, ministries and NGOs.

● The forum is based on a **Commission initiative of 2006** and is intended as an instrument for promoting the effective exchange of information and good practices, as well as **establishing a network** of the stakeholders in the field of protecting children's rights, be they governmental or non-governmental organisations.

● The discussion at the **first meeting** focused on the **role of the judicial authorities** in safeguarding and fostering children's rights. In particular, the protection of children against violence and sexual exploitation were the key topics of discussion.

- The experts discussed **repressive and preventive concepts to combat child pornography and paedophilia.**

- For example, the presentation of the **Berlin** approach of therapeutic primary prevention of child abuse of Berlin's University Hospital Charité attracted a lot of attention. This is a unique **therapeutic project** for the **prevention of child abuse** which became widely known in Germany because of a media campaign with the motto "do you love children more than you'd like?" As a result of this campaign, several hundred men volunteered for therapeutic treatment. The aim is to offer and investigate the effectiveness of preventive treatment for men with sexual impulses towards children before they act upon them.

Another focal point of the Conference was the presentation of the **achievements of legal prosecution** in the field of **Internet child pornography**: The public prosecutor's office of Halle, Germany, is conducting a criminal investigation against thousands of people worldwide who have ordered child pornography products on the Internet and paid for them by credit card. In cooperation with credit card companies, it was possible to identify them. For the first time all German credit cards (more than 20 million) were checked for certain search criteria, such as the payment of a certain amount of money and a transfer of this amount to a certain company.

A final declaration was issued at the end of the forum. The declaration encourages the development and implementation of strategies to promote the rights of children at the national and international levels, especially for the effective implementation of the United Nations Convention on the Rights of the Child. The benefits of close cooperation between all the stakeholders of the Forum were stressed so as to derive mutual benefit from existing good practices and exploit synergies.

2. Killer/Violent videos

At the initiative of the German Presidency, an initial exchange of opinions took place at the informal meeting of Justice Ministers in Dresden in January with regard to the increasing dangers posed to young people due to their consumption of killer and violent videos. They decided that further work should initially focus on clarifying the various rules in the Member States.

A report with the responses of the Member States to a detailed questionnaire was presented at the JHA Council meeting last week. With this, the Member States have a comprehensive compendium for the first time, which contains both the legal foundations and legal practice.

Last week, the EU Justice Ministers agreed to take additional steps based upon this work. They brought up Europol, which already has experiences in this field and could take action in cooperation with national bodies to protect children throughout the EU. It was announced that the debate would continue during the Portuguese Presidency.

Below are the activities of the German Presidency within the context of the EUCPN.

3. European Crime Prevention Network (EUCPN)

The EUCPN was set up by Council Decision 2001/427/JHA in May 2001. The main purpose of this legal act was to create a platform for EU Member States to exchange experiences, knowledge and best practices in the field of crime prevention. The wider underlying rationale was to promote crime prevention activity in EU Member States.

a) About EUCPN in general
The EUCPN's principal activity is information sharing. It provides a means through which valuable good practice in preventing crime, mainly volume crime, can be identified and subsequently shared between Member States. The basic idea is that the Network will support the development of contacts and will thus facilitate cooperation between Member States. Thereby it is intended to contribute to developing local and national strategies on crime prevention.

In this context it is important to emphasise that the EUCPN does not necessarily deal with all kinds of crime prevention activities. In mid-2005 the EUCPN National Representatives agreed in their Board meeting that the focus should be on three well-defined types of crime: juvenile, urban and drug-related crime.

b) EUCPN Best Practice Conferences
Much of the information exchange is done by way of seminars and conferences, such as the Best Practice Conferences. Once a year, typically in autumn and organised by the "Autumn Presidency", a Best Practice Conference is held that provides each country with the opportunity to present crime prevention projects in a certain field of delinquency. A particular topic is chosen for the conference, such as "alcohol-related crime" or "domestic violence", and then all National Representatives are called upon to look for promising, innovative and successful prevention projects in this field on the national level. Each Member State is allowed to nominate one prevention project as candidate for the annual European Crime Prevention Award (ECPA). Representatives of the individual - most often local - projects are invited to attend the Best Practice Conference, present their project and discuss their ideas with representatives of other national candidate projects as well as with EUCPN National Representatives.

c) EUCPN Website
The exchange of information, notably of best practices, is however not only done on the occasion of conferences and seminars; the EUCPN website (www.eucpn.org) also plays a major role in exchanging best practices in crime prevention.

Since fairly recently, the specific crime prevention policies of Member States for various specifically defined policy areas can be viewed and compared on the EUCPN website. So far there is information available to all users of the website on domestic violence, prostitution and trafficking for the purpose of sexual exploitation, public perceptions of safety and sexual crime.

Information on persistent offenders, vehicle crime, robbery and youth crime will be added soon.

d) German Presidency in the EUCPN
Finally, to summarise the efforts made by the German Presidency in the EUCPN: The EUCPN underwent a serious crisis a few years ago. Structural issues as well as a lack of resources were the main problems the EUCPN was confronted with. Against this background, the German EUCPN Presidency initiated an internal progress check of the EUCPN. A questionnaire was developed and disseminated to national EUCPN representatives with the aim of identifying possible deficiencies in the EUCPN and its structure. Its underlying rationale was to find out what is currently working well in the EUCPN framework and - maybe even more importantly - what is not. The results of this questionnaire, which we will have in December 2007, will serve as a first step for improving the EUCPN's structure, its visibility, the effectiveness of its activities and for communicating best practices in crime prevention in general. The next step in this process will be an external independent evaluation building on the results of the internal inquiry, since only external evaluators will be sufficiently neutral and inde-

pendent to identify all the issues that might be important. The independent evaluation is due to start at the end of December 2007 and is scheduled to finish in 2008.

Another reason for the EUCPN's crisis was a lack of academic input and of secretarial support to the EUCPN. Therefore, the German Presidency ensured that an interim academic advisory board to the EUCPN was established (interim "Research and Validation Committee"). Its purpose is to provide academic advice to the EUCPN and to verify whether the best practices meant to be communicated, are sound and valid. Since it is always difficult to find proficient experts for academic advice who are also available and have the time to support these kinds of activities, it was felt that the EUCPN's academic advisory board was in need of secretarial and research assistance itself in order to make it capable of completing the kind of work the EUCPN board was expecting it to do. Consequently, the German Presidency managed to secure the services of a knowledgeable young researcher based at Vienna University who is now providing sound and steady support to the Committee, both in an academic and an organisational way.

The most important event of the German Presidency in the EUCPN was an international one-day seminar on "Dangers of the Internet to Children and Juveniles". It was held on 1st June 2007, taking place on the premises of the German Federal Criminal Police Office ("Bundeskriminalamt"). Based on a multidisciplinary approach, it was the intention of the seminar to highlight the various concepts existing in the disciplines of media education, medicine and crime prevention. As far as crime prevention in a strict sense is concerned, different national concepts were presented by speakers from Germany, Sweden and Finland. There were six presentations, followed by a panel discussion where the speakers exchanged their views. The seminar was hosted by Mr. Carl-Ernst Brisach, President of Division "KI" of the Bundeskriminalamt, this division being the Institute of Law Enforcement Studies and Training. Mr. Brisach also chaired the panel discussion.

The first presentation was held by Mr. Thomas Rathgeb of the Media Education Research Institute of Southwest Germany. The topic of the presentation was the relevance of the Internet for young people's lives and new aspects of youth culture. Subsequently, Professor Jo Groebel, of the German Digital Institute, presented his research on "New Media, New Opportunities, New Risks and New Types of Delinquency in the Information Society". Dr. Andreas Hill, from the Institute for Research into Sexual Behaviour and Forensic Psychiatry at the University Hospital Hamburg-Eppendorf, reported on the effects of pornography in the Internet from a medical point of view, inter alia addressing the issue of addiction. He was followed by Ms. Ann Katrin Agebäck, director of the Swedish Media Council, who spoke on the Swedish prevention approach. Ms. Mari Laiho, who works as a project officer with Save the Children Finland, presented the Finnish approach to the issue. Finally, Mr. Reinhold Hepp, executive director of the Programme for Police Crime Prevention on the Länder and Federal Levels, completed the session by explaining the preventive approach taken by German police authorities.

From the perspective of the Presidency, the following conclusions were drawn from the seminar:

- The increased use and increased importance of the Internet brings great opportunities, but it also comes with considerable dangers, particularly for children and juveniles.

- However, this does not mean young people should be prevented from using the Internet. On the contrary: It is of special importance that dangers are not caused by lack of knowledge. Accordingly, improving "media competence" should be strongly encouraged, both for parents and for youths.

- Finding answers to the dangers of the Internet for young people is not only the responsibility of governments. It has to be a joint effort of the entire society: Besides the police and the justice system, parents, schools and particularly those offering Internet services are called upon to make active contributions.

- A promising approach has to be multidisciplinary in nature, involving media education, science, medicine, psychology, sociology, criminology, the justice system and the police.

- A profound exchange of knowledge and experience between these disciplines is needed. Yet, exchange is also needed between different nations, since the Internet, by its very nature, is a cross-border medium.

- The research done on the issue of Internet dangers is still insufficient. In particular, research needs to be done into the characteristics of risk groups and how to get messages across to them. Also, the areas for possible synergies between the various players need to be identified, and research needs to be done on the preventive effects of improved media competence.

Against the background of what has just been reported on EUCPN activities during the German EU Presidency, the question raised at the beginning: "Is the EUCPN now consolidated and is it a model for the future?" should be addressed. Quite naturally, this question is very difficult to answer. Taking all aspects into consideration, considerable structural and organisational progress has been made. This progress has brought back some stability and a considerable degree of seriousness to the development of the EUCPN. Regardless of whether the EUCPN is already a model for the future in its current shape, it will need our joint efforts to make sure that it will at least become a model for the future, building on the lessons to be learned from the EUCPN's internal progress check as well as from its upcoming external evaluation.

Contributions from participants at the 1st Annual International Forum

Tiina Ristmäe

Neighbourhood Watch as an effective crime prevention method in Estonia

Useful Concepts

Neighbourhood Watch (NHW) - A Neighbourhood Watch (also called a crime watch or neighbourhood crime watch) is a citizens' organisation devoted to the prevention of crime and vandalism within a neighbourhood. It is not a vigilante organisation, since members are ex-pected not to directly intervene in possible criminal activity. Instead, Neighbourhood Watch members are to stay alert to unusual activity and contact the authorities.

Neighbourhood Watch sector – an area (apartment block(s) or private houses) where people are organising Neighbourhood Watch.

Neighbourhood Watch leader – a person who is elected from Neighbourhood Watch sector members and who represents the Neighbourhood Watch sector in relation with other coopera-tion partners.

The Association – Estonian Neighbourhood Watch Association. This is a non-governmental organisation (NGO) which is organising and developing Neighbourhood Watch movement in Estonia.

Introduction

Neighbourhood Watch is well-known community action where people's communication and cooperation helps to create safe a living environment. The implementation of Neighbourhood Watch varies in different countries but the common keyword is the role of community mem-bers. It is a theory whereby everybody has a duty and opportunity to act towards safer homes. In this article the author gives an overview of the Neighbourhood Watch movement in Esto-nia. The first section describes the history of Neighbourhood Watch and in second, there is a description of how Neighbourhood Watch works in Estonia. In third section there is informa-tion about the results of Neighbourhood Watch in Estonia and the last section describes the difficulties faced during the implementation of the actions.

1. History of Neighbourhood Watch.

Neighbourhood Watch, as it is known today, began in the United States in the 1970s in order to combat the escalating rate of crime. In 1981 similar schemes began in the United Kingdom. The Neighbourhood Watch concept is widespread within the western world, particularly the USA, Canada, UK, New Zealand, Singapore and Australia.

The Neighbourhood Watch scheme in the United Kingdom is a partnership where people come together to make their communities safer. It involves the police, community safety departments of local authorities, other voluntary organisations and, above all, individuals and families who want to make their neighbourhoods better places. It aims to help people protect themselves and their properties and to reduce the fear of crime by means of improved home security, greater vigilance, the accurate reporting of suspicious incidents to the police and fostering a community spirit. The UK's first Neighbourhood Watch was set up in 1982 and 10 million people are now claimed to be members of different Neighbourhood Watch schemes.

1.1 Estonian Neighbourhood Watch movement

The Estonian Neighbourhood Watch had its roots in people's fear of crime and their desire to protect themselves. The Estonian NHW model was developed, following the UK's example. The model has changed over the course of time, and through the influence of local conditions and has achieved the necessary approach which works well in Estonia.

ENHW is an association, founded on May 5th, 2000 as a civic initiative, whose goal is to increase of sense of security of in and around homes by the inhabitant's own active practice of Neighbourhood Watch. This was the citizens' reaction towards the dramatic cut of the number of police officers in 2000. The primary aim of this organisation is to raise interest among inhabitants of private houses as well as apartment buildings towards Neighbourhood Watch and to inform them of the goal, principles and potential of Neighbourhood Watch.

To achieve this aim, the Association facilitates the forming of non-governmental associations and movements dealing with Neighbourhood Watch and supports their activities, introduces principles of Neighbourhood Watch, publishes print-outs and carries out training, and develops cooperation with state and municipal governments, police and other institutions.

The task of the Association is to be an organisation that unites non-governmental associations and people dealing with Neighbourhood Watch, to share information and training with its members. The Association acts on behalf of its members in finding partners and in the development of cooperation with them.

2. How does Neighbourhood Watch work?

The first condition of starting Neighbourhood Watch in a district is that people should realise that they both need and want to participate in this movement. If the initiative comes from the police or the Association, then they probably start with NHW but the activity might not be so effective. So if there is initiative within one area then it is important that they receive adequate information about NHW. Usually the people organise a meeting and the representative of the Association (with police if possible) comes to introduce the potential of NHW. Then people can decide – is this what they need and do they want to participate in NHW?

If they want to join a NHW, the first step is to gather their data – name, address, e-mail, telephone number(s), car number and colour. Each participant confirms with his/her signature that they agree to the using of this data in NHW activities. After the meeting there is enough time for everybody to sign on to the NHW scheme if they are interested. It is of course possible to join or leave the scheme at a later date. This data will be updated at least once a year but usually after each new member joins or when somebody leaves the NHW scheme.

The members of NHW sector choose a leader who will represent them in the cooperation agreement, in NHW meetings and who will be a contact person for other institutions. One further obligation of the NHW sector leader is to update the data of NHW members.

2.1. Neighbourhood Watch cooperation agreement

Once the data of the NHW members is gathered, the next step is to sign the contract. It is a c-operation contract between four (in Tallinn five) parties - NHW sector, the police, the local government and the Association (in Tallinn also the Municipality police). The contract is a joint agreement that we all make an effort to promote greater safety in this area and we work in close cooperation. The contract is signed by the highest ranking person in each party – NHW sector leader (elected by the members of the NHW sector), the mayor, the head of the district police and the managing director of the Association. The process of contract signing is very important to people who have just joined the NHW. They can see that their activity is noticed and recognised at the highest level of authorities and of course it is a good opportunity to discuss the possible solutions to the problems which the NHW sector might have.

2.2. What happens after the agreement?

After the contract signing the members of NHW sector will receive a folder, which contains a different kind of advice-leaflet and information booklets about safety. Furthermore there is a document with the contact details of their neighbours and some information about our coop-eration partners in the field of safety.

The Neighbourhood Watch sector members are given signs by the Association, so that strangers can see that people living in this particular area are observant and will react if they see something suspicious.

2.3. The actions of Neighbourhood Watch members

The main principle of NHW is that if you see something suspicious, you do react. How does one know how to react? How does one know when to call the neighbour, the police or the local government? Usually new members of NHW have such questions. To answer those questions and give basic information about safety, the Association organises training. This meeting, where all the members of the NHW sector are invited, is usually held shortly after the signing of the agreement. The Association, the police and the local government send their representatives to the meeting to share information and answer questions. If neighbours weren't familiar with each other previously, this meeting is a good opportunity to get to know each other.

2.4. The document with contact numbers.

As mentioned in paragraph two, members of NHW sector give contact details to the NHW sector leader. The Association makes a document with the details of neighbours, police, local government contacts and Association contacts. All emergency numbers are included as well. This document helps the neighbours to know how to react if there is some kind of problem. For example if a member sees a stranger in his neighbour's garden, he can make a call to the neighbour and share this information. If it is clear that there should be nobody in the garden, they will call the police and a possible theft will be prevented. Or another example from the apartment building, where one women notices that there is water dripping from the ceiling. She goes to the upstairs neighbour's apartment but they are out. She has the neighbour's contact details in her NHW folder, so can make a call to prevent worse damage. Those examples are from everyday life and could happen to anybody. Usually we tend not to notice such things (first example) or we can do nothing and just wait for neighbour (second example). In Neighbourhood Watch it is important that you NOTICE and then you REACT. Learn to notice comes with time and experience but also by following the example of other people. The basic information about how to react is shared in the first training meeting of the NHW sector and whenever the need for new knowledge appears.

Being part of a Neighbourhood Watch should be integrated into each member's everyday life. There are not many extra duties or obligations for a NHW member. The NHW sector leader is a contact person for other cooperation parties and if there are meetings, this person is invited to represent the NHW sector. Once a year the Association organises a general meeting where all the NHW sector leaders are invited. This is a meeting to develop the Association and to discuss future activities.

2.5. Neighbourhood Watch patrols.

Usually it is the opening question in NHW's first meeting "do we have to start patrolling?" In Estonia patrolling has a very small part in the NHW movement. It is not very common to see NHW patrols in the Neighbourhood Watch area. However, there are some sectors where patrols are organised. The Association supplies them with patrolling vests, the local police give a short basic training - what to look for and how to react. The idea is that NHW patrols are the eyes and ears of the police, if they notice something where intervention is necessary, they will call the police, but shouldn't intervene themselves. The police are aware of the NHW sectors where people go patrol. Patrolling is voluntary and the Association supports the initiative of NHW members.

3. The impact of the Neighbourhood Watch movement in Estonia.

Neighbourhood Watch has been practiced in Estonia for about seven and a half years. The members usually feel and notice the results of their activity but what is the overall impact? Is NHW an effective model for reducing fear of crime and preventing crimes? To get answers to those questions the Association ordered surveys from the University of Tartu. The first survey was conducted in 2004, and the second in 2006. In 2007, the Ministry of Justice conducted the audit of the Association' activities during the period of 2003-2006. The next survey by the University of Tartu is planned to take place at the end of 2008.

In the study which was conducted by the University of Tartu the author describes the latest survey which was conducted in 2006. The aim was to find out how the members of NHW sector evaluate the effectiveness of NHW, how they rate the cooperation with the police, the local government and also the Association. Also we wanted to know suggestions for future activities.

The target group was selected from the biggest areas where NHWs operate – Tallinn city, Harju and Viljandi county. The sample consisted of 283 respondents (members of different NHW sectors) who were interviewed by telephone. The questionnaire included 36 questions which were divided into different sections.

The first section gave an overview of how the respondents evaluate the NHW in terms of crime prevention. 67% of respondents said that their home has become safer after starting with NHW. 72% believe that help is now closer than before. 18% of respondents know that in their sector a crime has been prevented, while 10% know a case where the action of NHW has helped to catch a criminal. This should be considered a very good result considering how rarely we actually witness a crime. Also this data is not available anywhere else, as the police only records crimes committed, not the prevented ones.

The second section of the interview concerned relations between neighbours. 13% of respondents said relations have improved after starting NHW. The rest reported relations remained the same. The third section described the actions of the NHW sector. 48% of respondents have helped to improve safety within the NHW sector (new locks, safety doors, gates, patrolling etc).

We also asked about the motivation to participate in NHW activities. The main motivation is the need but demonstrated results are also important. So if all is peaceful and there are no problems, people do not need to think about NHW, it is integrated in their everyday life. This seems a good result since NHW shouldn't be guarding and watching but rather acting when intervention is needed.

The survey also gave information about relations between the NHW sector and the police and the local government. 20% of respondents think that the cooperation with the police has improved. But most of the respondents consider the cooperation with the police to be at the same level as before the NHW participation. Cooperation can not be one-sided and there is enough room for development for both the police force and NHW members.

Cooperation with the local government is occasional and many respondents do not actually know anything about it. This is also a field where improvements are necessary. The last section of the survey was about the need for training. Almost every respondent indicated the need for some kind of training – 83% of respondents request training in how to act in an emergency situation, 75% need training about law enforcement legislation, 71% need information about how to make their home safer (technical possibilities) and 71% need more information about how to improve NHW activities in their district. This is the actual working field for the Association because one of our aims is to offer varied training to our members. But there is one problem that makes it difficult to satisfy the need for training. In the research there was also a question about the time to take part in this training, and it emerged that only half of the respondents actually have enough time to take part in the training. So we can not draw conclusions here that organising training will improve the quality of NHW activity, because many people simply do not have time to participate. But this is a subject where the Association has to find a solution with NHW members.

To sum up the survey, the results show that NHW helps to prevent crime and reduce the fear of crime. The members of NHW know that the necessary help is closer and if necessary, they can cooperate with their neighbours. The Association coordinates the work of the NHW sector - the main duties are counselling, organising training and compiling information documents. The unique cooperation model of local people, the local government, the police and organisation who coordinate the structure has received the support of all parties and is effective in preventing crime and reducing the fear of crime.

A brief note about the audit of actions which was conducted by the Estonian Ministry of Justice in autumn 2007. The Ministry of Justice has supported financially the Association's actions and the main aim of this audit was to find out if the work which has been done with their support has been effective and had a positive influence on the target group. The auditor studied the reports of the Association's work between 2003-2006, interviewed the managing director of the Association and also conducted a survey among NHW sector leaders. The auditor's final report suggests that Neighbourhood Watch is an effective method to prevent crime and to increase the safety in one community. Furthermore, Neighbourhood Watch gives people the opportunity to change their community positively, and not just to wait for somebody else to act. The auditor recommended continuing the implementation of NHW.

The Association has tried to get crime statistics from the police as well, but this is complicated because of the structure of the database. Unfortunately it is therefore not possible to relay on police statistics and analyse the effect of NHW. Still, in 2006 one police officer in Lasnamäe, a city district of Tallinn, made a comparison between two apartment houses. The blocks were situated closely to each other and both had 90 apartments. In one block there was

NHW, in the other there was not. The block with NHW had no crime against property during the period of January- December 2005, whereas the other had 7 offences. It is not possible to draw deep conclusions from this example, but this is here just to support the surveys described above.

4. Difficulties in implementing Neighbourhood Watch.

The text above can lead to the impression that NHW is the magical solution for every problem. But crime still exists, people become victims and that also happens in NHW sectors. When considering the difficulties in implementing NHW in Estonia we should start with Estonians' values, attitudes, history, traditions and nature. We are developing from a society where everything was organised and people should not, or actually were not, allowed to intervene in the functioning of society. Society in Estonia has now been organised differently for some decades, but many people still think that somebody else is responsible for the individual's life, actions and safety. People say that we have police and safety companies – they work towards our safety, so why is Neighbourhood Watch necessary? This is the mindset of many people in Estonia and no-one else but themselves can change this belief.

One problem that we have noticed is passiveness and a lack of knowledge. It concerns the values – what is important and how one tries to live one's life. It is noticeable in everyday life in traffic, in relations, at work. It is hard to change this attitude and it can also damage the positive enthusiasm of others. But here it is possible to draw a parallel with school atmosphere – if the majority have a positive attitude towards learning in a classroom, and the main values are friendship, helpful and empathic relations, the whole class has a positive atmosphere. In society generally, it is the same, so the solutions in this case would be a more positive example to follow.

The third difficulty is related to the development of nongovernmental organisations and it may be that these problems are specific to Estonia. It regards financing crime prevention programmes, and financing the implementation of all the activities which are mentioned in this article. NGO Estonian Neighbourhood Watch budget consists of different financial sources: 50% from local governments, 30% from the Ministry of Justice, 10% membership fees and 10% sponsorship. The state thinks that NHW members who participate and benefit from the movement should contribute 50% towards its budget. On the other hand, the NGO offers a service – an effective crime prevention programme which is the only of that kind in Estonia. Should the state have a long term contract with NGO since crime against property has the largest share of criminal offences (63% in 2006)? Or should the local government pay for this, as the direct user of the service? Those questions are raised every year and there is no straightforward answer. Still we have chosen to adapt our actions to the current situation and we are working towards better conditions both for us and for other NGOs who are in a similar situation.

Conclusion

In Estonia there are 365 Neighbourhood Watch sectors and 9862 members of NHW (10.12.2007). Over the course of seven years, the organisation has found a place in Estonian society and now people turn to it to find information about NHW, whereas just a few years ago NHW sent members around door-to-door, to ask if people would be interested in joining. It shows that NHW is necessary and helps to fill a place in society where neighbours can get to know each other and work in cooperation.

It is said that Estonians are big individualists, who tend to prefer being alone rather than working in a group. Our experience shows that although it is difficult to start, with good leadership and common goals there can be really positive and effective cooperation.
The key to the success of NHW is cooperation and the exchange of information between house/apartments owners, the local government and the police. Living in an apartment building or private house where you know your neighbours and have contact with them, you can be sure that in case of trouble they can help you.

If neighbours know each other, social control increases among the inhabitants – it is more embarrassing to misbehave if all the people are acquainted. Kids and young people would probably also behave when they realise that everyone knows their parents.

Communicating with the neighbours certainly gives many good ideas about how to make the staircases, playgrounds, parking lots or cellars a safer place. If the whole neighbourhood supports someone's idea, it gets a wider base and it is easier to put it into practice.

NGO Estonian Neighbourhood Watch has changed significantly since the beginning. Now that more attention is accorded to the quality of NHW sectors, the number of sectors is not of primary importance, compared to how they work. Also the organisation has become the only means of representing people's interest in safety and crime prevention, we are unique not only in Estonia but also in the whole world. So we are an influential partner for national and local government, police as well as security, insurance and lock companies.

In the future the NHW movement should receive greater attention in society since the people's role in creating safer living environments is increasing. But they need some tools to start caring for their homes and communities. They need the chance to act on the lowest level – their home, neighbourhood, but also the highest – state and government level. The NGO Estonian Neighbourhood Watch gives them the opportunity. It just takes some activity, caring and willing!

Resources used:
1. Wikipedia, the free internet encyclopaedia
2. The survey among Neighbourhood Watch participants, 2006. www.naabrivalve.ee Available only in Estonian

3. The audit of actions conducted by Ministry of Justice, www.justiitsministeerium.ee
   Available only in Estonian

Crime in Estonia, 2006. The publisher: Estonian Ministry of Justice

Contacts of the organisation:
NGO Estonian Neighbourhood Watch
Tatari 12
Tallinn 10116
Estonia
Telephone: +372 6522522
Mobile phone: +372 51 36630
Fax: +372 6522522
Webpage: www.naabrivalve.ee / E-mail: info@naabrivalve.ee

Anna Karina Nickelsen

Crime Prevention in Denmark - Current status

The following is a brief overview of the Danish approach towards crime prevention. Bearing in mind that The Preventive Council of Denmark is undergoing a transforming process, the Danish Preventive Council will have a new structure and a new strategy from 1st November 2007.

In Denmark the citizens don't worry excessively over crime and they generally have a significant sense of being safe and secure. The reasons for this feeling of safety and security are, of course very complex.

The way that the Danish society has actually worked with crime prevention since the 1970s is based on the idea that crime prevention is primarily a social responsibility. 20 percent of the population even finds crime prevention to be one of the most important tasks of the police. On the other hand, every member of society is expected to contribute. Accordingly, the basis of the Danish crime prevention is the cross-sectoral cooperation between the public and the private sector. Even individual citizens are supposed to take responsibility and act in the interest of the community to prevent crime.

Focussing on the public sector, the cooperation between the different parts of public administration is essential and may be the core of the Danish idea of crime prevention. Accordingly, the co-operation in the public administration will be the main subject of my overview.

Multidiciplinary cooperation

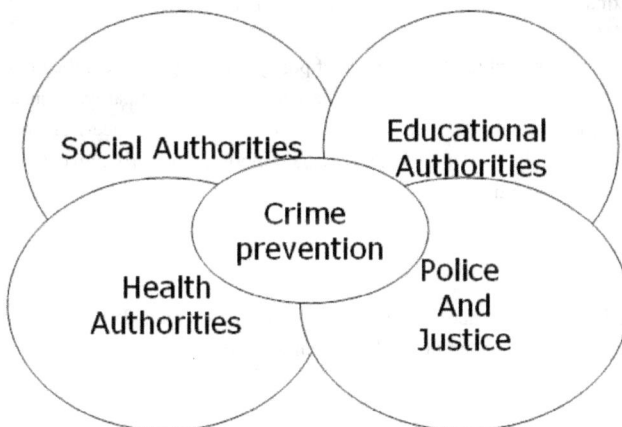

Social prevention, health, education and publicity work are all publicly acknowledged to have a crime preventative effect. But crime is a smaller part of the problems that a person might face. Issues of social affairs, health and educational politics are part of the political agenda at the national level when crime is discussed. There are however political trends to introduce more severe punishments to prevent crime. But for some years, crime preventative measures, such as community service, social treatment of juvenile delinquents, conditions of treatment for drunk drivers' alcohol abuse, and cognitive programmes for violent criminals have been part of the sanctions used in Denmark.

To this day it has not been necessary to make a clear distinction between crime prevention and e.g. social prevention.

At a practical level, crime prevention is in my opinion, most commonly understood as the area where the responsibilities of the different authorities overlap. What do we do with the risk behaviour of kids? What do we do with violence among kids? How do we avoid violence in families? etc.

The Danish municipalities

Denmark is divided into 98 municipalities.

The services of the municipalities are often divided into Children and Culture Service, Social Service, Road and Traffic etc. The primary and secondary schools are part of the Children and Culture Service.

The municipalities in Denmark have a legal responsibility to prevent crime. The purpose of the law on social service is, for example, to offer counselling and support to citizens to avoid social problems. Crime is considered to be a severe social difficulty. The municipalities have the responsibility to find the right kind of care, to offer it and to pay for it.

The municipalities are also obliged to make a coherent policy for children. The policy is supposed to cover all sides of the activities of children and youth in the municipality, to ensure a preventative and early intervention, flexibility and coherence among the services. The policy should, for example, describe the role of kindergartens and schools in the early prevention and intervention for vulnerable children.

SSP Cooperation, etc.

Today, local cooperation between school, social services and police - called SSP cooperation - is the cornerstone of local crime prevention work with children and young people.

Social authorities

School   Police

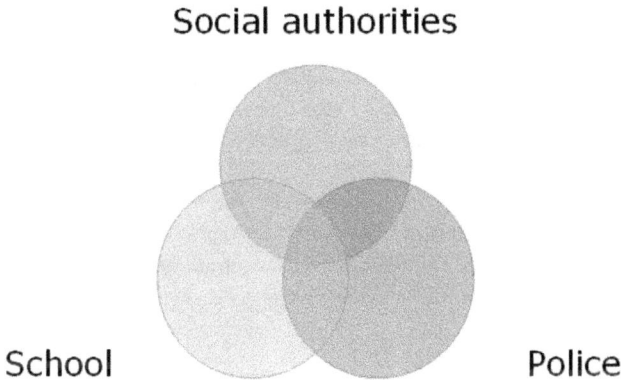

The aim of SSP co-operation is to build, use and maintain a local network that has an influence to deter crime and criminal behaviour in the daily life of children and young people. SSP cooperation provides an opportunity for the early detection of danger signals, and new trends in crime development and the conditions of life for children and young people, so that measures can be taken to prevent them from taking a criminal path. At the same time, SSP cooperation is well suited as a forum to clarify which preventative options exist locally for the authorities involved. SSP co-cooperation can also instigate projects to prevent the emergence of groups or gangs of young people with criminal behaviour.

SSP co-cooperation also deals with young people over 18 (called SSP+). Accordingly, SSP+ is an important link in crime prevention efforts to cooperate with local businesses to find apprenticeships or workplaces for young people who need special supportive efforts on their behalf.

SSP co-cooperation between the police districts and the municipalities should be developed even further with emphasis on close cooperation with each local authority in the police district. Furthermore, more generally, it would be natural to consider the future organisation of crime prevention efforts, including the work under the auspices of SSP.

As part of future local crime prevention efforts, the police commissioners should also take the initiative for each police district to prepare a special plan for strategic crime prevention actions regarding children and young people in the district. Such a general strategic plan could include the following topics, among others:

-       A systematic course of *general efforts* made during the childhood and adolescence of children and young people with the involvement of schools, clubs, and other places dealing with youth education. Such efforts could include information campaigns, special SSP days, regular meetings between SSP employees and the police and parent boards of children's day care institutions and schools, joint activities as part of school projects, etc.

- *Specific efforts* aimed at groups of children and young people at risk of developing criminal behaviour. These efforts could, of course, be implemented in co-operation with local father groups, schools, youth clubs, etc., and fieldwork on the street.

- *Individual-oriented efforts* for young people who have already committed a crime, with a view to preventing recidivism. These efforts could involve actual treatment or attempts to establish new social relations for these individuals outside their usual environment, for example, in cooperation with the local business community about traineeships, etc.

District Councils

Local Crime Prevention

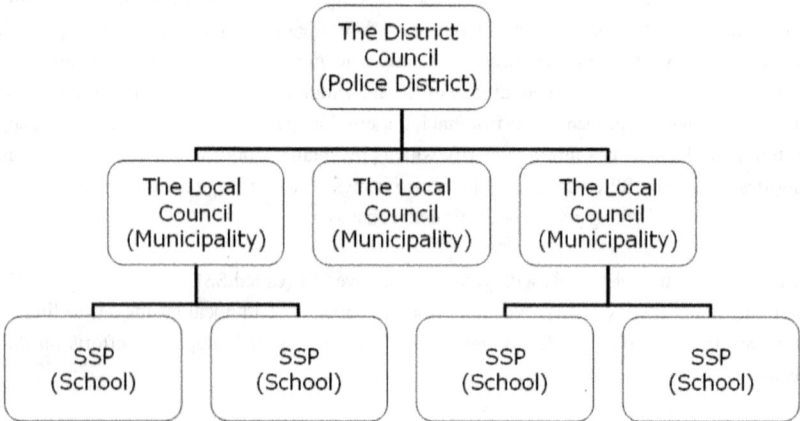

A new *district council* has been established, as of January 1st 2007, in each police district. The district council is composed of the police commissioner and the mayors of the local authorities, comprised by the police district. The district council will thus serve as the central executive forum where the chief executives of the police and the local communities have an opportunity to discuss issues of common interest.

With a view to underlining the police commissioner's independent responsibility for planning police cooperation with the local authorities in the police districts, the police commissioner is appointed chairman of the district council in the police district. The mayors concerned should represent the local authorities.

With a view to underlining the function of the district councils as the central contact forum for the chief executives of the local police and the local authorities, it has been decided that the district councils shall meet at least four times a year. Naturally, the district councils can hold more meetings as required.

The district council shall discuss all issues of a general nature regarding the police's activities and organisation in the police district. It is particularly relevant to discuss areas where there is a need to ensure cohesion in the undertaking of tasks by the police and the local authorities, for instance with regard to the efforts made on behalf of children and young people at risk. The district council shall discuss organisational issues of special importance to the local community, e.g. changes in station districts and opening hours, etc.

The district council shall furthermore discuss crime development and local crime prevention etc., in the police district, and this could most frequently take place based on the police's analyses of the nature, extent and development of the crime problems in the different parts of the police districts.

The district council shall try to give local people information about the police's activity in the district, including crime prevention initiatives, for example.

The police commissioner shall submit one yearly written report to the district council regarding the police's activities in the past year. This occur, e.g. in connection with the police district's submission of its annual report to the district council. It would be prudent if, in addition, the police commissioner prepares status reports and the like for the district council regarding the general police efforts in the district and/or concrete efforts in specific focus areas.

The district council may submit statements about issues regarding the general organisation of the police district and the district council can recommend to the police commissioner that for a limited period of time the police shall prioritise solving special tasks with regard to upholding safety, peace and order in the police district.

Local Cooperation Plan

It is important for all relevant local players in the new police districts to become involved in cooperation in the tasks best solved in collaboration between the police and the local community.

In order to further anchor and strengthen this involvement, the police commissioner shall prepare a total *plan for cooperation* between the police and the local authorities, other public authorities, interest organisations, associations, etc., in the police district.

The police commissioner should prepare the local cooperation plan for one year at a time after prior discussion in the district council. Thus the district council shall take up the plan once a year with a view to ensuring that it always provides the best possible framework. The plan is to be published, for example, on the website of the police district. In this way, it would be possible to use the cooperation plan as a reference for the local community and as an inspiration to other police districts.

The local cooperation plan should contain a more detailed description of how local cooperation is or will be organised and implemented in the police district. The plan should address the most important local cooperation areas, including local crime prevention cooperation between the police and the individual local authorities (SSP cooperation, etc.). Aside from that, there is a very free framework for how the police commissioners, in consultation with the district council, will draft the cooperation plan. In connection with the current follow-up on the cooperation plan, new important cooperation forms and forums could be included in a revised plan.

Role of the community police

The 12 Danish police districts are divided into an investigating department, a department prepared for action, and the community police.

The community police are helping to ensure close contact between the police and the local community, including the local authorities. The community police are posted at the different police stations (headquarters and the other police stations) in the police district, and the daily leader of each community police unit is able to prioritise and use the resources of the local police in the best possible way, given local preferences and requirements, within the framework set out by the management of the police district. The head of the community police in each police station is the contact person in the day-to-day work for the local authority concerned, including in connection with local cooperation on crime prevention (SSP cooperation, etc.)

The Danish Crime Prevention Council

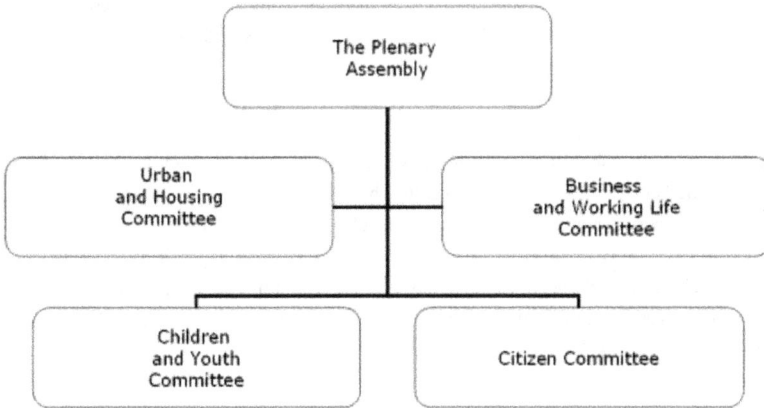

```
                    ┌─────────────────────┐
                    │    The Plenary      │
                    │     Assembly        │
                    └─────────────────────┘
                              │
        ┌─────────────────────┼─────────────────────┐
┌───────────────────┐        │        ┌───────────────────┐
│      Urban        │        │        │     Business      │
│   and Housing     │────────┼────────│  and Working Life │
│    Committee      │        │        │    Committee      │
└───────────────────┘        │        └───────────────────┘
             ┌───────────────┴───────────────┐
┌───────────────────┐            ┌───────────────────┐
│     Children      │            │                   │
│    and Youth      │            │ Citizen Committee │
│    Committee      │            │                   │
└───────────────────┘            └───────────────────┘
```

The Danish Crime Prevention Council is a national committee.

The council is a public – private partnership, or network. The council has approximately 50 members e.g. researchers, the police, the ministry of education, the ministry of social affairs, the association of municipalities, the association of producers of security equipment, the association of insurance companies, and trade unions of policemen, social education workers and schoolteachers. The council is supposed to be a mirror of the Danish society.

The council works at national level. The aim of the council is to prevent crime and create a safer and more secure society through a coherent and effective approach to crime and crime prevention. The council should define national crime problems in need of attention, and identify ideas of intervention. The collaboration in the council provides the members with an opportunity to coordinate their knowledge and their efforts and provides the members with an opportunity of informal dialogue with relevant partners.

The council is about to establish 4 new standing committees:
- The Children and Youth Committee
- The Citizens Committee
- The Urban and Housing Committee
- The Business and Working Life Committee

The target groups of the council are the members themselves, the district councils and the public.

A secretariat of 25 employees – some of them with degrees in law, criminology, psychology, pedagogical science and communication - facilitates the collaboration in the council and is responsible for the public information and other public activities of the council.

Conclusion

Since the 1970s, Danish crime prevention has been based on a bottom-up approach. The core element of the Danish idea of crime prevention has been – and still is – cooperation between authorities, and between authorities, the private sector and the citizens.

In recent years, Denmark has been designing and implementing very radical reforms moving tasks from national to municipal level as well as merging police districts from municipalities to larger units.

A small part of these reforms has been establishing the district councils and the local councils with the purpose of strengthening the strategic part of local crime prevention, and the communication between the bottom and top in local administration.

A decision has been made to evaluate the police reform. Part of the evaluation is, for example, a study of the existing and future cooperation between the police and the municipalities regarding crime preventive work.

At the same time the Danish Crime Preventive Council has increased its focus on timing and effective methods, process and coherence.

In Denmark the results of these adjustments in the Danish Crime Preventive approach are eagerly anticipated in a couple of years.

Janina Czapska

Crime prevention in Poland 18 years after the transformation

1. There is no general or abstract normative rule (act, decree), which would regulate the issue of crime prevention in Poland. There is neither a bill nor any political initiative in this field. However, it does not seem that such a normative act is necessary. The sphere of responsibility for security in Poland is characterised by the diffusion of competence and the duties in the field of preventive actions are set out in various normative acts (see further). Such a state of affairs makes it difficult to establish a clear division of competence and responsibility. In order to amend the law it is sufficient to make particular acts more precise.

If a centre for coordination of prevention, so necessary in Poland, were established on the basis of existing regulations through decisions issued by central administrative bodies (which seems feasible), then solving this matter by means of legislation, as sometimes suggested, would be unnecessary.

Another argument supporting the passing of a general normative act is the need to regulate the legal status of subjects dealing with prevention as well as to define statutorily the sources of financing preventive actions. In the context of the reality in Poland, it is important to consider the necessity to regulate the principles for the financing of preventive activity.

I am opposed to granting special powers to citizens conducting crime preventive actions in organised groups in their local neighbourhood. Members of such groups should be given the rights of the so-called man on the street (the right to act in self-defence and in higher necessity, as well as to detain a perpetrator caught red-handed).

The task to prevent crime has been statutorily assigned to the following subjects:

- the Act on the Police passed in 1990 art. l section 2 defines the fundamental tasks of the police. Although the commentators of the act criticised the imperfect formulation of the tasks of the police, it is generally felt that its tasks as regards crime prevention have been relatively well stated. Among the seven most crucial tasks the legislator stated in point 3 are the "*initiation and organisation of activities aiming at prevention of perpetration of criminal offence and misdemeanours as well as crime stimulating phenomena and cooperation with state and self-government bodies and public organisations in this field.*"

- the act of 1997 on communal (municipal) guards specifying their task to perform duties in the field of public order protection resulting from acts and regulations of the local law (art.10 section 1) rules among others the necessity of "*informing local community about the state and types of dangers as well as initiating and participating in activities aiming at prevention of perpetration of criminal offence and misdemeanours as well as crime stimulating phenomena and cooperation -with the state and self-government bodies and public organisations*"

- the tasks in the field of crime prevention have been also assigned by statute to bodies of territorial self-governments. Since the democratic principles concerning the organisation of territorial authorities were reactivated in Poland, the powers in the field of order and public security have been divided between state and self-government bodies.[1] These tasks can be performed by a self-government which can undertake actions or make use of their powers as regards the state police. The self-government is perceived mainly as a potential source of financing and coordinating activities, development or rebuilding of infrastructure and technical means of communication. The territorial self-government's tasks concerning the providing of security to the citizens have been – since 1990 (the act on a territorial self-government) – broadened many times which justifies submission of a proposition about progressive communalisation of security in Poland as particularly essential changes were introduced in 2001 in the result of the administrative reform of the country carried out in 1998. Communes (basic level of territorial self-government and the tripartite administrative division of the country) should provide security to citizens as a part of their fundamental tasks. They may do it by establishing their own services like communal guards (compare previous point). The *poviat* (the second level of the administrative division of the country and self-government) self-government is burdened with the most important tasks. The *poviat* council was obligated in 2001 to adopt a *poviat* programme of crime prevention and protection of citizens' security and public order. In the aforementioned renewal of the act on territorial self-government a new institution responsible for public order and security was introduced – a commission for security and order. As assumed, these commissions should perform functions similar to prevention councils in other countries but mostly they restrict their activity to the performance of minimum of the statutory tasks or even only activities of symbolic character. They are extremely rarely a creative factor as regards issues of public security. The adopted solution making the commission an advisory and consultative body of a *starosta* (an executive body of a territorial self-government on a *poviat* level) instead of a body coordinating the public security system was totally wrong.

On the basis of the analysis of the normative acts in force, one may state that the issue of crime prevention is also discussed in other normative acts, like the Act on Public Prosecutor's Office, Juvenile Crime, Province Offices' Statutes. These shall not be closely discussed in this paper, as they do not introduce duties of specific bodies in the field of prevention.

In Poland few books have been published on crime prevention. Many books are not available because of the place of their publication and the limited circle of addressees as is in the case of publications (very often handbooks) in the Police High School (the only Police High School in Poland)[2] Significant books were published by the Institute of Public Affairs (non-

---

[1] Recently: R Głowacki, K. Łojek, Zagadnienia prawne policyjnych działań zapobiegawczych. Wybrane aspeckty (Legal Issues of Police Preventive Activity. Selected aspects), Szczytno 2005.

[2] For example : R. Głowacki, K. Łojek ; Zagadnienia prawne policyjnych działań zapobiegawczych. Wybrane aspekty. (Legal Issues of the Police Preventive Activity. Selected aspects) Szczytno.

governmental organisation). They primarily contain the texts of the speeches on crime prevention delivered during the International Self-government Workshops organised in Krakow in 1998, 1999, 2000[3] and the results of the study of the Research Unit on the Reform of the Police and Common Security, working in this institute from 1997 to 2000.[4] Only three monographs devoted to his matter have been published.[5] It is worth mentioning that there are publications co-written by both scholars and policemen.[6] Moreover, one needs to mention a number of articles published by academics in legal or criminological magazines as well as police press articles prepared by police journalists or experienced policemen.[7]

2. Many countries have appointed special committees at a central level to coordinate prevention, promote the best programmes and finance local initiatives. They are carried out at the Ministry of Justice, Home Affairs etc. Establishing such a body would certainly facilitate the exchange of information and strengthen the effect of positive examples which are spread through the entire country. On the basis of the analysis of the solutions adopted in other countries and the situation in Poland, one might consider whether it would be useful to establish a new subject to deal with the coordination of the activities in the field of prevention on a central level. In Poland the state and self-governments do not take full advantage of the possibilities that could occur through the cooperation of state and non-state subjects as regards security. The causes for such a situation are both of objective and subjective character. Considering the present state of legal solutions, we should, first of all, include among objective causes, legislative drawbacks which do not allow the explicit determining of legal principles of cooperation (e.g. a very general regulation on cooperation). Among psychological barriers there are mainly simplistic thinking, belief in the ineffectiveness of actions or about their purely symbolic character, or finally a general lack of understanding. In such a situation the establishment of a nationwide organisation might improve that cooperation. Among the reasons for the failure of efforts so far, mainly undertaken by the Police Headquarters, is the fact that social and especially political awareness associates the prevention of crime, similarly to repression, with the police and their duties. The influence of politics on the issue of security, which is not typically Polish, makes decision makers, and parliamentary politicians especially, inter-

---

[3] J. Czapska, W. Krupiarz (ed.), Zapobieganie przestępczości w społecznościach lokalnych (Crime Prevention in Local Communities), Warszawa 1999; J. Czapska, J. Widacki (ed.) Bezpieczeństwo lokalne. Społeczny kontekst prewencji kryminalnej (Local Security. The Social Context of the Crime Prevention), Warszawa 2000; J. Czapska, H. Kury (ed.) Mit represyjności albo o znaczeniu prewencji kryminalnej (The Myth of Repression or: the Importance of Crime Prevention), Kraków 2002.

[4] J. Widacki, M. Mączyński, J. Czapska (ed) Local Community, Public Security, Central and Eastern European Countries under Transformation, Warszawa 2001.

[5] A. Bałandynowicz, Prewencja kryminalna (Crime Prevention), Warszawa 1998; T. Cielecki, Prewencja kryminalna (Crime Prevention), Opole 2004, J. Czapska, Bezpieczeństwo obywateli. Studium z zakresu polityki prawa (Citizens' Security. A Study in Legal Policy), Kraków 2004.

[6] In 2007 a 3 volume work was published on selected aspects of the police and self-government activity in the field of providing security, also in the form of preventive actions.

[7] In 1998 inspector T. Cielecki (Ph.D.), the former police commanding officer of Kielce province, conducted a survey in all province and regional police stations in Poland. The subjects of the survey were specialists on crime prevention.

ested in striking ideas and often, populist slogans. Another argument is based on drawing attention to the fact that crime prevention must remain local so any central body is redundant. The misunderstanding results from a different view of centralised bodies, which opponents regard as an organ administering prevention centrally in Poland – and we have bad memories of such bodies from the past.

In the 1990s the Chief Headquarters of the Police prepared a project to establish a body to coordinate activities in the field of crime prevention on a central level, however, it has never gained enough political support. It seems that a National Forum for Crime and Pathological Phenomena Prevention should be established with non-governance powers which would deal with finding professionally prepared educational material etc., as well as promote the best ideas, and therefore it should inform and coordinate, educate, inspire local preventive programmes, monitor the initiatives already in place, make information available about the situation in Poland and abroad, and incorporate Polish activities in this field into the 'European Crime Prevention Network'. The Forum might organise research and prepare and assess legal regulation projects and even independently prepare long-term programmes to improve security in particular spheres e.g. prevention of violence in schools, and make expert reports commissioned by state organs or commission other people to prepare such reports.[8]

In Poland two national (central) programmes to provide security have been established in which prevention played a crucial role. The State Programme for the Improvement of Citizens' Security of 2002 was a comprehensive proposition to improve security in the country. Ministers of Internal Affairs and Administration, Justice, Finance, Economy, Labour and Social Policy, Treasury, Education and Sport, Science and Culture and National Defence have been obligated to act within this programme. It was supposed to ensure the improved cooperation of the Police and public prosecutors' office, and create conditions to act effectively for them. In this respect the programme had to be assessed critically, as those 'conditions' were mainly limited to information, though positive effects of the annual 'Safe Commune' competitions must be emphasised, in which territorial self-government institutions carrying out particularly valuable projects in providing security received financial awards. The successive rounds of the competition enjoyed greater and greater popularity, measured by the number of entrants. It was a form of financial support for local prevention initiatives although the instructions for granting awards raised some controversy. It was a form of awarding programmes which were already being realised, as only programmes that had been going for at least three months were evaluated. There was no initiative for financing the best projects thus giving inspiration through contracts. Among controversial propositions included in the programme 'Safe Poland', an idea to regulate 'citizens' guards' by a statute must be mentioned.

---

[8] cf. J. Czapska, Bezpieczeństwo, p. 297-298.

In December 2006 the Prime Minister unexpectedly signed a new resolution of the Council of the Minister which set up the government programme to limit crime and antisocial behaviour 'Safer Together', which will be realised in 2007-2015.[9] 3m zloty (about € 810.000) a year were allocated for the realisation of the project. Emphasis is placed on the creation of integrated local communities. For example, in the second half of 2007 particular attention was drawn to such issues as town security maps and forming housing estate groups, domestic violence, and security in schools. The chief coordinator is the Minister of Internal Affairs and Administration who is assisted by representatives of the Chief Headquarters of the Police and selected ministries. Throughout the country the activity of working teams should be coordinated by *voievodes* (or province governors, executive bodies of the highest level of the administrative division of Poland). Also the intensification of cooperation within EUCPN (European Crime Prevention Network) is being contemplated. Among the initiatives mentioned in the programme, the establishment of the bank of Good Practices must be praised. This will help self-governments, citizens' organisations and territorial units of the Police to find programmes useful in their area. Another positive point of the programme is the budget allocation for donations to organisations of public utility and the co-financing of local self-governments on the basis of the agreement between state and self-government administration for projects related to security. It is worth mentioning that the programme provides for it being monitored and evaluated. Due to the short period of time which has passed since the programme was created, it is difficult to assess its performance. It seems that too important a role has been assigned to the representatives of the Police, which may in future lead to their dominance in the realisation of these programmes. Moreover, it is doubtful whether the Ministry of Internal Affairs and Administration is able to ensure the effective coordination of activities. In the system of crime prevention in Poland it is important to realise that particular ministries gained much autonomy, which favours rivalry. What is more, problems with coordination appear between the Police and self-governments[10].

The realisation of that programme falls within the period of return to centralising tendencies in the organisation of the Police. Moreover, nowadays the Polish Police base their vision of work on the theory of 'authoritarian intervention and symbolic justice'. That stage in the development of the police is critically described as 'symbolic cooperation with society' which means that the police expect society to provide both initiative and assistance, being themselves interested only in their image in the eyes of society.[11] Turning the Police off the road to decentralisation and union with a self-government within the so-called mixed model and re-

---

[9] http://razembezpieczniej.mswia.gov.pl/. It is difficult to foresee the fate of the programme in connection with the victory of former opposition in the parliamentary elections.

[10] In Poland, being a uniform country, there exists one state Police.

[11] T. Cielecki, Koordynacja systemu zapobiegania przestępczości przez samorządy lokalne (Coordination of the System of Crime Prevention by Local Self-governments), w :A. Szymaniak (Ed.) Samorząd a Policja. Kształtowanie bezpieczeństwa lokalnego (Self-government and the Police. Shaping Local Security.), Poznań 2007, p.36-37.

treating to a centralistic model becomes a decisive factor in the obstruction of social and self-government initiatives over cooperation with the Police.[12] For example, provisions allow for concluding an agreement between self-government organs and the police concerning financing by the former of a post of a district constable for a period of minimum 5 years (compare point 4). From 2000 – 2003 self-governments transferred means to finance 740 posts, and at the same time in the police *poviat* units, the number of district constable posts was gradually reduced by 1355[13] to increase the number of the patrol and reactive policemen.

The difficulties in the realisation of tasks in the field of crime prevention also arise from the attitude of policemen towards it; less than a half of the policemen consider preventive activity most important when providing security is concerned, 10% consider it totally worthless and 20% do not think such activity to be important.[14]

3. The Police are the first to be included in the group of players dealing with crime prevention. Apart from them, either individually or in cooperation with the police, other non-government organisations, the Catholic Church, municipal guards, informal citizen organisations, local self-governments are engaged in prevention. The potential of private security firms for the protection of people and property is still exploited only to small extent although (rare) successful attempts are evident. For example in Kraków since 2002, a quality certificate for the best private security firm for the protection of people and property has been awarded. The principle of the competition is to stimulate private security firms working in Kraków to act in support of activities improving citizens' security. The aim is to choose the best working firms which assist the city in its attempts to improve security. The certificate confirms the high quality of the services provided and particular engagement in strengthening citizens' security in cooperation with the city.

As the result of preventive actions undertaken by the police, we can observe greater cooperation of the police with other subjects. According to the policemen surveyed in 1998 - specialists in prevention - the cooperation between educational and healthcare units is best arranged, between territorial self-government bodies and public prosecutors and courts. 30% of the respondents positively evaluated the cooperation with social welfare and 40% the cooperation with the church and administrators of houses and flats.

General information is scarce about actions undertaken by non-government organisations, government and self-government administration, specialised educational and healthcare units. Making the actions of various subjects autonomous is highly disadvantageous, impedes or

---

[12] T. Cielecki, Koordynacja, p. 40.

[13] T. Cielecki, op.cit., p. 37.

[14] B. Hołyst, Psychologia kryminalistyczna (Criminal Psychology), PWN 2004, s. 1363. It seems that such attitudes are the result both of the training as well as the practice In the evaluation of the policemen's work used by superior officers and units.

successfully hinders preventive actions. The lack of sufficient information makes policemen who deal with prevention undertake spontaneous preventive actions, instead of ensuring co-operation of specialists in a given field.

In Poland there is a lack of reliable and up-to-date information about the number of prevention programmes being implemented and their effectiveness.[15] Police programmes are relatively well known. From 1991 to 2000 the Police Headquarters in provinces handed several descriptions of various programmes on prevention to their units, ranging from individual ones the complex project "Safe City". Implementation of pilot projects for prevention began in 1993. The police project "Safe City" has been conducted in the whole country with varying intensity since the beginning of 1995. The project included some suggestions for preventive actions, defined principles, forms of activity and its structure. It primarily recommended to respect the principle of founding projects on surveys of needs and threats in local communities. It addressed cities, communes and residential areas. Within the framework of the "Safe City" project a variety of subprojects are conducted depending on local needs. The most fundamental goals of the projects can be analysed on the basis of their names: Safe Home, Street, School, Business, Residential Area, Fun, Holidays, Relax, Neighbourhood Watch (the Neighbourhood Project to Counteract Crime), Police Educational Project in Schools. Preventive projects also concern fighting alcohol abuse, monitoring of dangerous places, influencing mass media, managing children's and young people's free time.

Province structures of administration, the police and other participants were to hold coordinative meetings due to the lack of a government body to coordinate an interdepartmental combat against crime. The concept of the "Safe City" project corresponds with the standards applied by well-known British projects, for instance The Safer Communities Partnership, The Strategic Partnership, The Safer Cities Project. The initial 9 year period of implementing crime prevention activities in Polish police – quite consistent in the theory phase – was not so consistent in the realisation phase. Despite various ups and downs, the programmes recommended by the Prevention Bureau of the Chief Headquarters for province headquarters appeared to be quite consistent, beginning with the presentation of strategy, then dispersed initiatives and finally comprehensive long-term prevention programmes. However, the implementation of those propositions appeared to be much worse. Sometimes that period is quaintly described as 'leaflet prevention' because on the most part the activities consisted of preparing information materials on different subjects related to security (mainly the flat, public transport, car parks and the road to school).

---

[15]According to the T.Cielecki's report, in 1998 the police in Poland were carrying out 1268 preventive projects. They were conducted by 80% of regional and province police units. The full complex "Safe City" projects were carried out by 10% of police units, more than 8 projects by 5%, from 5 to 8 by 20%, from 1 to 4 projects by 44% of units.

In 2007 in relation to the state programme 'Safer Together', the Police introduced a programme called 'Safe Cities', in which they plan to intensify their activities in small and medium-size towns in the following spheres on the basis of threats identified in the research conducted this year in January: security in public places and residential areas, in schools, means of public transport, on roads and in running a business activity.[16]

The preventive projects conducted nowadays in Poland have two basic aims: to inform and to educate. A gradual transfer towards projects of a new generation, with wide scope, clear planning and assessment elements can be seen, but they are still exceptions in comparison to the programmes duplicating errors of prevention programmes described comprehensively in world literature; occasional actions, the lack of good diagnosis prior to the selection of the programme and the lack of an evaluation of the course of the action and its effects.

Poland has relatively large number of school educational projects. One can define these as typical for primary prevention. Their form varies from typical meetings with young people or children in the classroom, meetings with children in small groups with the use of tapes, films, colour books and to drama shows for kindergarten children. Children also have an opportunity to participate in interesting meetings with policemen or guards in the form of a play. All of them are to serve the children's preparation for defence against different dangers. Education of teachers and parents is another supplementary element. In some centres preventive programmes are devoted to combating drug abuse among young people. Unfortunately, we are not familiar with any attempt to evaluate them.

Among preventive projects, education of adults in the risks of victimisation, establishing confidence telephones by the police is distinctly less frequent. The percentage of projects counteracting concrete risks in specific areas is surprisingly small. It is rare to encounter: tackling dangers in stadiums, burglary at summer houses, taxi drivers' self-defence, and prevention of poaching. There are few projects notified for enhancing security for the elderly. Relatively speaking, the marking of bicycles is more frequent.

Some of the projects conducted in Poland were directed to improve security and order in specific regions. They comprise creating secure zones, squares and similar places. Their common aim is to ensure security in certain parts of cities. In appointed regions the number of police patrols, often together with municipal guards. During meetings with inhabitants, dangerous zones and ways of liquidating them are specified, lighting is improved, places of special danger monitored, other subjects are encouraged to improve security and order. The essence of these projects is comprises of two elements: intensive patrol control and using district constables according to their duties specified within the framework of *community policing* theory.

---

[16] Policyjny program ograniczania przestępczości i aspołecznych zachowań w małych i średnich miastach „Bezpieczne Miasta" (The Police programme to limit crime and antisocial behaviour in small and medium-size towns 'Safe Cities'), Warszawa 2007.

Introduced in October 1998, one of the most complex projects is the system of police domestic intervention called "Blue Cards". This is a project to counteract domestic violence allowing the supplementing of police actions with real preventive procedure carried out by a district constable accompanied by social services units.

As has already been mentioned here several times, the most dominant among the realised preventive projects are those which are of an informative and educational nature. They need to be categorised as typical means of primary prevention, i.e. directed towards society as a whole, as potential victims or perpetrators, less often directed towards changes at community level. Decidedly fewer projects belong to secondary prevention, and prevention directed to perpetrators or victims of crimes is exceptional. Neighbourhood Watch projects, together with secure zone projects or reorganising the function of a district constable, can be rated as means of both primary and secondary prevention.

Second Generation CPTED is becoming more and more popular though as far as the implementation of this programme is concerned, one can make a thorough study of the weaknesses of Polish activities. The research projects are being carried out by 5 universities of technology and the Police High School, the results of which are publications, scientific conferences, a supervision of implementation as well as cooperation with the Police in selected cities. The Integrated Project for Security, realised on the basis of Dutch experience by the Police in Kraków in cooperation with several universities in that city, became an illustrative example. However, this issue is only hinted at in the programme 'Safer Together'; it is also omitted In the coordinating actions of the Chief Headquarters of the Police: nor doest much information unfavourable towards innovation reach the local self-governments. Programmes referring to CPTED are only implemented in some places mostly where the there is a long tradition of cooperation between the Police, self-governments and academics.

4. In 1991 the Police Headquarters announced new strategy for counteracting crime, prepared a year earlier. Although it referred to preventive activities within the framework of criminal law and penitentiary prevention as of prime importance, it also very strongly stressed the necessity for a parallel development of activities within situational and social prevention. According to the police concept it was agreed that a district constable would fulfil the basic preventive function in local communities. The strategy also referred to the experience of Western European countries. A district constable should be the most basic player who is responsible for cooperation with local communities in order to prevent crime. This would be a police officer of so called first contact, serving in a specific area. In November 1997 the Police Commander in Chief appointed a team to introduce the project "My district constable". The project included the idea of building a new model of a district constable, a manager of the area of duty, who makes close contact with community. The basis for that was the order of the Chief Police Commanding Officer in 1995. In 2007 a new regulation was issued concerning 'forms and methods of performing tasks by a district constable and the supervising officer of district constables.

Each new Chief Police Commanding Officer aims to restore the function of a district constable, so far without much visible success. Out of a 100,000 policemen in Poland, we have approximately 9000 district constables. According to the modest evaluation, in order to realise the function of a protector of a certain district, there should be about 16,000 of them. The lack of success in creating a real district constable implementing the idea of *community policing* in the Polish police results from several fundamental causes.

Self-governments have so far shown friendly interest in supporting this institution, however without concrete actions, especially in the sphere of financing. As of January 1st 1999 the legal situation changed so much that the new regulations provide for financing additional posts of district constables by self-governments for at least 5 years on the grounds of the agreement concluded with a province police commanding officer. Until mid June 1999 there was one such agreement concluded, although a number of self-governments expressed their interest in such possibility. Reducing the number of municipal guards and designating the money saved in this way for additional posts in the police has become an undesirable phenomenon on a national scale. Unnecessary rivalry appeared. Policemen race to diminish the expenses of their actions, only to distance themselves from the expenses of maintaining municipal guard and to take over money designated for them. This is not the way. Both services, the police and guards could perform a number of duties provided they cooperate reasonably. In the situation where the role of a district constable has not been sufficiently specified, such a change of a guard into a policeman may lead to the situation where some of the duties of ensuring order in a commune will be left without adequate provisions. Undoubtedly, such an attitude was accepted by the representatives of territorial self-governments since the tendency ended after two years and at present in Poland, the number of communal guards formed optionally by self-governments is growing.

One of the causes of failure connected with the introduction of the new model of district constable is the notorious imposition of additional current tasks on them (for instance to conduct preparatory proceedings), which impedes the realisation of preventive functions in their districts,[17] the lack of stability of the job caused by personnel fluctuation which leads to difficulty in getting properly acquainted with their district, acceptance by local society, anonymity of a district constable, all of which destabilise the system of professional training.[18] Moreover, the attitude of many district constables is not without significance as they, perceiving the low prestige they enjoy in the Police, treat their function as a temporary stage to a career in the inquiry and investigation section.

---

[17] The findings of the report of The Prevention Bureau at the Police Headquarters indicate that approximately 50% of work time of a district constable is devoted to duties which require them to leave the borough.

[18] M. Stefański, Rola dzielnicowego w procesie kształtowania poczucia bezpieczeństwa (The role of a district constable in the formation of the feeling of security), in: A. Szymaniak (Ed.) Samorząd, p. 150.

The third element which must be underlined, is the incorrect training of district constables in Poland which results in the lack of competence and skills which are necessary to carry out preventive projects. As long as a district constable neither enjoys an appropriate position in the Police hierarchy nor has motivation to work (prestige and remuneration), it is difficult to expect a breakthrough in the treatment of a district constable, who has been described in the press as 'rubbish-bin for everything'.[19]

5. Citizens' commitment to preventive projects can be arranged it various ways.[20] One of the typical ways is the participation in the Neighbourhood Watch (NW). In Poland at the beginning of the 1990s they were mostly organised by the police; later such activity was also carried out by communal guards and self-governments. Examples were mostly taken from Great Britain. According to surveys conducted among policemen - specialists on crime prevention – in 1998, 44 out of 1268 projects were the Neighbourhood Projects to Prevent Crime. This is very few, however one has to consider that the qualification criterion has an extremely formal character[21].

It is not possible to define what part of Polish society is involved in similar initiatives. As research shows, more then a half of Polish people declare to provide neighbourhood help in defence against victimisation (55% in 1995 and 61% in1996). It is not easy to state what part of these declarations mean more than the friendly watch of a flat or an exchange of conventional courtesy. Prevention projects aim to prompt people into a friendly interest in their neighbours, to break anonymity, to undertake collective actions in order to improve the standard of living in the closest surrounding neighbourhood. Except for the simplest conventional actions this is the behaviour that people should learn. Such education might be supported by the high confidence that the Police enjoy in society.[22] The Polish people's attitudes towards preventive activities are incoherent because they simultaneously involve supporting groups of neighbours' assistance, and expressing the expectation that the state, to which we pay taxes, should act and protect us effectively.

I am not in favour of creating paramilitary groups in the form of institutionalised citizens' patrols.[23] I oppose providing prevention groups with special rights. Members of groups should

---

[19] M. Dębicki, Marzenia dzielnicowych (The District Constables' Dreams), Gazeta Wyborcza z 8 października 1997.

[20] If citizens were asked abort the most frequently implemented preventive measures, they would most often point to passive forms of behaviour , for details compare J. Czapska, Private Initativen als Mittel der Kriminalitätskontrolle In Polen, In: J. Obergfell-Fuchs& M. Brandenstein (Ed.) Nationale und internationale Entwicklungen In der Kriminologie, Festschrift für Helmut Kury zum 65. Geburtstag, Frankfurt 2006, p. 507-508.

[21] Only the projects which have been precisely named as such by their creators and participants have been included to the Neighbourhood Projects. Possibly many other preventive projects, which have not been named as neighbourhood ones, are also based on co-operation of inhabitants.

[22] For details compare. J. Czapska, Private, p. 531-532.

[23] On the subject of citizens' patrols and their history compare J. Czapska, Private, p. 511-516.

have the rights of the so-called every man: the right to self-defence, to act in the state of higher necessity, to detain the perpetrator *in flagrante delicto*. With the extension of their rights without any training or after a short course, a serious danger may rise due to the limited possibility to control their conduct. While exercising special rights or transgressing them in the case of intervention, members of paramilitary groups constitute danger for other citizens, for bodies of security and order, and finally for themselves. In the meantime the support for such initiatives in Poland must be taken into account, which resulted from the specific under-standing of the principles of a democratic state by some citizens and is especially disturbing in this context. In the aforementioned government programme 'Safe Poland', legal regulation of citizens' guards was planned as an important element of the social support for the security activity. These plans ended in only a catalogue of regulations which may give legal grounds for functioning of such forms of citizens' self-organisation in the light of the binding law. It did not come to the legitimisation of citizens' paramilitary groups by the state in the form of a new law regulation.

6. Cooperation with foreign partners has existed since 1990. It was mainly seen in the training of Polish specialists on prevention, as well as in foreign visitors to Poland who assist the prac-tical realisation of specific projects in our country. In the process of the training of the Polish police, Great Britain's assistance project which has been conducted since 1990 within the framework of The Know-How Foundation has been of essential significance. Considering the fact that most of the domestic and foreign training has initially been based on our British con-tacts, it is not surprising that many of the approved solutions in Poland were similar to the British solutions. Moreover, Polish policemen have visited the United States, France, Ger-many, The Netherlands etc. Policemen from Chicago taught Polish policemen in two big pro-vincial cities how to organise police actions in CAPS system. The educational program for children called 'Live Normally' first conducted as a pilot project in Chełm, and later also in-troduced in other regions of Poland, has been realised according to Dutch models. Danish SPP project served as the basis for partial preventive actions in Kielce. In the former province of Zielona Góra the Dutch police assistance in the organisation of prevention has led to joint street patrols of Polish cities. Permanent cooperation has existed between The Dutch Police Institute in the Hague and the Police Headquarters in Warsaw. Common preventive actions have been conducted with our Eastern neighbours.

The input of foreign experience into the creation of strategies for preventive activity in Poland has been well documented by one of the Police Commander in Chief's advisors. A. Przemyski paid attention to the fact that at the beginning of 1990s we used foreign models, adapting them to Polish conditions. Today on the grounds of ideas worked out in other countries, the

Polish police are trying to find their own methods of acting.[24] Thus joint research projects undertaken by Polish researchers and policemen together with foreign partners within the framework of European grants are of great importance.

Despite positive evaluation of European cooperation for the development of research and activity in the field of crime prevention, it is necessary to point to fundamental difficulties, which encompass:

a) the lack of coordination of actions undertaken by various subjects, both at the central level where different departments are responsible for particular aspects of prevention; Ministry of Education, Ministry of the Internal Affairs and Administration, Ministry of Health and Social Welfare, and subjects acting in one specific area,

b) the lack of stable and transparent forms of financing of preventive projects

c) the lack of ready methods of evaluation of realised projects, and therefore "everyone has to learn a lesson".

In order for crime prevention to be successfully conducted in Poland, there are several fundamental conditions to be fulfilled. Firstly, it is necessary to establish a new model of a district constable, implementing the idea of *community policing* in local communities. The need to reform the police education system is connected with it in order to introduce crime prevention as one of the subjects of training at an elementary level, as well as a series of training for specialists on prevention at all levels of police structure. Secondly, it is necessary to alter the law regulation of the commissions for security and order in *poviats* to take better advantage of the knowledge of the experts employed in them. Thirdly, it is important to establish a system of monitoring preventive actions, and relations with citizens, especially with reference to receiving information about crime. Next, it is vital to allocate larger sums of money for prevention or at least to establish permanent sources of financing of preventive actions and clearly determine the principles of allocating them to stimulate local initiatives in the field of crime prevention. Finally, it is necessary, as stated earlier, to appoint an organisation to coordinate the policy of counteracting of crime and serve as the centre of information and exchange of experience.

Crime prevention is a subject of increasing popularity in Poland. With a little exaggeration one could almost say it is becoming fashionable. It takes many years of reasonable and successful education to create citizens who are aware of their partial responsibility for security, and that sometimes even the simplest precautions may greatly increase security. It will take a

---

[24] A. Przemyski, Community policing po polsku (Community Policing the Polish Way), in: J. Czapska, W. Krupiarz (ed.) Zapobieganie przestępczości w społecznościach lokalnych (Crime Prevention in Local Communities), Warszawa 1999.

long time before we see these effects. If only one could make politicians take interest in the status of prevention, we could support this process with supplementary propaganda actions. Success in this sphere is hard to achieve because certain politicians reveal tendencies to undertake short-lasting and more striking action, and as said before, prevention of crime is fundamentally a cooperative work.

Libor Gašpierik[1] and Jana Müllerová[2]

Criminological aspects of delinquency of juvenile and criminality of teenage offenders in the Slovak Republic

I would begin by saying that I am glad to participate in this international conference and I would express conviction, that its results will be beneficial also in conditions of the Slovak Republic.

Interest in practical solution of problems that are related to criminality and its prevention can be seen in Slovakia recently. It appears from the state and structure of criminality and from reality that criminality is one of the most severe social-pathologic phenomenon of Slovakia. Criminality prevention must react to its state; it must go from concrete conditions and react to its causalities.

Important attributes which must be protected by every society are internal order and security. It is not sufficient to be aware of that. What is extremely important is to convince exsisting society with one's own achievements of ability of all interested to build a well-ordered society in which unlawfulness will be replaced by lawfulness and where lives, health, possession, rights and liberty of citizens will be protected. In real life this especially refers to security and protection against criminality of all kinds, criminals and offenders of minor criminality, producers and distributors of drugs, persons that endanger moral education of juveniles and infringers of public order.

Slovak Republic government also considers criminality prevention as a basis of criminal policy of the state. In the present it prepares basic controlling document "Strategy of criminality prevention and other antisocial activities in the Slovak Republic" which will be valid until 2010. The government has also an object to crown legislation process of historically the first criminality prevention law in 2008 where ministries and other concerned statutory undertakers participate under sponsorship of the Ministry of Internal Affairs. The government in its program declaration also declared that it will pay attention to social prevention as expression of solicitude for the most vulnerable groups of citizens and especially children and youth, elderly people, battered and abused women. Important is that the government declared financial support of prevention programs and that they will endeavour so that criminality prevention would be all-society affair [1].

---

[1] Senior Lecturer, MSc. Libor Gašpierik, PhD., Department of Security Management, Faculty of Special Engineering, University of Žilina, Street 1.mája 32, 010 26 Žilina, +421/41-513 6654, e-mail: Libor.Gaspierik@fsi.uniza.sk

[2] MSc. Müllerová Jana, PhD., Department of Technical Sciences and Informatics, Faculty of Special Engineering, University of Zilina, Street 1.mája 32, 010 26 Žilina,+421/ 41-513 6616, e-mail: Jana.Mullerova@fsi.uniza.sk

What is the situation of juvenile delinquency and criminality of teenaged offenders in selected kinds of crimes in Slovakia like?

The structure of criminal activity of young delinquents is created by typical crimes against property, bodily harm, fights, and criminality in transport including drunkenness, disorderliness, statutory rape, parasitism and unauthorized use of foreign motor vehicle. Increasing number of serious juvenile crimes should be considered as a warning signal. Greatest grow in criminality of children in comparison with adult offenders is seen in property criminality, and then it is violent crime. Juvenile delinquency is connected with group crime, alcoholism and nonalcoholic intoxication. Specific for juvenile criminality is vandalism.

Dynamism of whole criminality of the young in 1996-2006 dropped. The number of crime committed by the young decreased from 12 455 crimes in 1996 to 6 654 in 2006 (table 1), what is nearly a half fall of crimes. Mentioned decrease is relative. Development of these offenders portion on criminality detection rate which shows different tendencies shows evidence of it. We can talk about decreasing tendencies also after 1998 from which the rate of the young in crime decreased from 20% to 14% in 2006. Though on the one hand the young participated in more than one quarter of all clarified crimes in Slovakia on the other hand in the present the young participate in clarified crimes less than one sixth.

Development of juvenile delinquency shows different tendencies as development of whole criminality of the young. In 1996-1998 increase of juvenile delinquency was recorded which culminated on 5 000 crimes in 1998 (rise from 4 596 to 5 022 crimes). We can talk about decreasing tendencies from 2000 when number of crimes committed by these persons oscillated about 4 000 crimes and in 2006 decreased on 2 300 crimes what is in comparison with 1996 decrease about one quarter of crimes. Development of the young participation on total criminality in 1996 – 2006 was between 5 – 11 %.

We registered marked decrease in juvenile delinquency in 1996-2006; it was lower up to 55%. Dynamics of the rate of the young on total criminality in 1996-1997 oscillated on the level 17 – 18 %. After 1999 was marked decrease of the young criminality state seen also on decreasing rate of the young on total criminality, which in the present does not exceed 10%.

Tab. 1: Total criminality of the young in the SR in 1996-2006 [2]

	1996	1997	1998	1999	2000	2001	2002	2003	2004	2005	2006
Total criminality	99402	92395	93859	94016	88817	93053	107373	111893	131244	123563	115152
Clarified	45116	43642	45658	47067	47107	50818	55212	51683	51635	95204	47481
The young	12455	12349	11871	11145	9724	9528	9854	8759	8101	8158	6654
Juvenile	4596	4987	5022	4859	4159	3937	4131	3755	3149	3349	2364
Teenaged	7859	7362	6849	6286	5565	5591	5723	5004	4952	4819	4290

Violent crime is a part of so called general criminality. It includes mainly violence heading for other person but also against things and psychical violence. Impending actual application of physical violence can be motivated either hostility or it can be so called instrumental violence serving to other purpose. Between the young it is especially in form of blackmail or chicane which is typical for apprentice youth but they are often also in primary schools.

Structure of the most often cases of delinquency of this type is brigandage. It is typical criminality becoming to so called street and thereby metropolitan criminality of the young. The number of boys is higher than girls. They are mainly offenders from inferior social stratum. Recently the cases of the most severe criminality occurred, bodily harms with death following. The most of murders is emotive. The major are murders which are means to other objective. There is psychopathologic phenomenon, which burden appropriate adaptation surrounding social environment. Reasons of violence between the young are various. They are conditioned socially, culturally, economically, psychologically, physiologically but in some cases also politically.

Violent criminality of the young developed in 1996-2000 by similar way as violent criminality that means it had increasing tendencies. Increase in quantity of criminality of the young from 1 519 in 1996 up to 1 779 in 2001 represented 15% accrual. There was noticeable decrease after 2006 while the young people committed 862 crimes (tab. 2). From the view of development of violent criminality of the young it is needed to see mainly the development of violent delinquency of juveniles. The number of violent delinquencies committed by juveniles in 1996-2001 represents increase about more than 60%. That is regarding to the lowest age category the alarming fact. In 2002-2006 we register decreasing tendencies of the state of violent criminality while decrease from 939 cases to 342 in 2006 (except 2005 – increase to 678 cases) represents 274% decrease. Even though mentioned development in recent years can create optimistic prognoses it is necessary point that rapid increase of violent delinquencies of juveniles was multiple higher than following decrease in the number of violent crimes otherwise punishable.

Tab. 2: Violent criminality of the young in Slovakia in 1996-2006 [2]

	1996	1997	1998	1999	2000	2001	2002	2003	2004	2005	2006
Violent crime	11391	11564	12427	13531	13459	14450	15020	13724	13755	12906	10896
Clarified	9790	10146	11083	12137	12228	13192	12948	10353	9961	9526	7475
The young	1519	1544	1506	1667	1721	1779	1620	1316	1267	1478	862
Juvenils	555	568	683	730	926	939	776	562	532	678	342
Teenaged	964	976	823	937	795	840	844	754	735	800	520

Property criminality of the young

Property criminality is the most frequent part of the total criminality of the young. They are typical form delinquency of children and the young. They are more often in big towns than in villages. With higher age there is possible decrease of criminality of the young. Some property criminality is possible to consider as so called chivalrous delinquencies. The often reason of property criminality of the young is non filled leisure time and with this relating deviation to criminality.

Property criminality is the most common type of criminality and the most frequent group of criminalities committed by the young. Development of the number of registered cases of property criminality of the young (tab. 3) was the same with the development of total criminality of the young. From the table and the graph follows that property criminality of the young showed decreasing tendency. Regarding to the mentioned development of the state of property criminality committed by the young is an interesting fact that the rate of these offenders in clarified property criminality had in 1996-1997 conversion tendency that means it increased up to 50%. After 1998 there is gradual decrease of the rate of the young participation on this criminality up to present 31%.

In examination of reasons and condition of criminality of the young and at planning of preventing precaution is important knowledge that in the last century juveniles and young persons became between the most frequent groups of offenders participating on property criminality committing.

The development of property delinquency of juveniles was different from the development of the property criminality of the young. Between years 1996-1999 was the property delinquency about 3600 cases per year. Marked decrease of property cases otherwise punishable was markedly shown at the beginning of this decade while the present state is about 1600 cases. Juvenile offenders have high rate on property criminality which increased up to 20% level in 1997 what means that every fifth case clarified property crime was committed by persons younger than 15 years.

The state of property criminality of the young shows decreasing tendencies, while the number of property crimes of the young in 1996-2006 was decreased nearly more than one half. The rate of the young was lower up to the present 40% from 1996 what still means one fifth of all clarified property crimes.

In property criminality of the young as well as at their total criminality it is interesting that the state of property delinquency of juveniles and criminality of the young in comparison with the 90ties of the last century does not show marked differences what should be stimulation for other examination but also stimulation for effective prevention activities aimed mainly at children under 15 years.

Tab. 3: Property criminality of the young in the SR in 1996-2006 [2]

	1996	1997	1998	1999	2000	2001	2002	2003	2004	2005	2006
Property criminality	67772	62411	93130	60275	52923	54022	57543	61034	77098	65306	63077
Clarified	19442	19022	19851	18375	15660	16370	17486	16388	14415	13780	14803
The young	9553	9508	9097	8160	6714	6551	6880	6146	5608	5357	4632
Juvenils	3625	3912	3802	3561	2668	2524	2831	2710	2206	2251	1600
Teenaged	5925	5596	5295	4599	4046	4027	4049	3436	3402	3106	3032

Moral criminality of the young

It is non coherent whole of criminalities from which a part is in criminological dividing called as sexual criminality. Its basis is gratifying of libido by forms which are not tolerated by society. Crime refers to one or more persons. Rape and sexual abuse belong to criminality with high danger for society because they interfere in the field of human dignity but also in healthy course of young people. Sexual abuse in some isolated cases occurs with juveniles, they are predominantly committed by juveniles and children with the age close to juveniles. With girls it is mainly prostitution. In many of these cases it is for property purpose.

Development of moral criminality of the young is quite varying but in spite of this we record in dynamics of its state two culmination points. The first increase we record in 1997 where the number of criminalities committed by the young reached 335 cases. After 1997 we record mild decrease but in 2000 the state of moral criminality of the young again overstepped 300 moral crimes. So the years 1997 and 2000 are the culmination years in the field of criminality increase. Marked decreasing tendencies are seen in recent years, when the number of moral crimes committed by the young decreased fewer than 200 cases. Regarding to low number of moral crimes the more interesting criterion is the rate of young population on this clarified criminality (tab. 4). We determine that in the last decade were the young participating in moral criminality in high rate, while the rate of the young culminated in 1997 on 45% level.

In the next years 1998-2001 we recorded mildly decrease and the rate of juveniles and teenaged offenders on moral criminality oscillate on about 40%. Marked decrease was there after 2002 when the young participated in moral criminality in 30%. From the mentioned indicator we can claim that young people in the age of 18 have high participation not only on property criminality but also on one of the most serious social kind of criminality as moral criminality is.

From the view of juvenile offenders is alarming the progress of the rate of their participation in this kind of criminality. While in 1996 was the rate of juveniles on moral criminality only 10%, in the present it is 17% what is regarding to the kind of criminality and the group of offenders quite high representation.

Tab. 4: Moral criminality of the young in SR in 1996–2006 [2]

	1996	1997	1998	1999	2000	2001	2002	2003	2004	2005	2006
Moral Criminality	833	769	669	721	783	756	773	835	875	794	798
Clarified	796	731	645	685	750	723	672	653	713	626	589
The Young	333	335	270	271	301	284	235	197	218	217	218
Juveniles	79	111	104	86	119	91	86	73	106	83	101
Teenaged	254	224	166	185	182	193	149	124	112	134	117

Conclusion

The state and aims of solution of criminality prevention in the Slovak Republic are shown in the article. There is an analysis of the state of the selected kinds of delinquencies of juveniles and criminality of the young offenders in the article. Interest of all our society is so that our young generation could grow healthy and with positive attitude to abidance of rules. That is why it is very important to realize the aims we have in Slovakia. I hope today conference will help to fulfill this aim. Thank you for your attention.

Bibliography

[1]   Programme Declaration of the Government of the Slovak republic. Bratislava 2006.
[2]   SELKENKA, M.: Statistical Summary of Juvenile Criminality – Criminal Offences. Bratislava 2007.
[3]   GAŠPIERIK, L.: Criminology. Selected Prelections from Criminology for Students of Security Management. Žilina, FŠI 2003.
[4]   GAŠPIERIK,L.: Prevention of Criminality. Selected Prelections from Criminology for Students of Security Management. Žilina, FŠI 2005.
[5]   SEJČOVÁ, Ľ.: Behavioural Characteristics of Youth in the Slovak republic. Criminality Magazine 2002.
[6]   GAŠPIERIK, L. – PECKOVÁ, Ľ.: Selected problems of Criminality Prevention and Prevention of Other Anti-social Activities. Almanac FŠI ŽU of 12th International Conference. Žilina 2007.
[7]   BOC, K.: Fulfilments of Duties resulting from Strategy of Criminality Prevention in Slovakia for the Armed Forces. Almanac of Vocational Conference: Criminality Prevention and Armed Forces of Slovak Republic – Model 2010. Trenčín 2002.
[8]   VEĽAS, A.: Possibilities of Security Developments on Local Level. In: Science and Emergency Situations. Almanac of Prelections. Ostrava: VŠB – TU, 8.11.2005. ISBN 80-248-0944-3.
]9] TAKAĆ, T. - LOVEČEK, T.: Employment of Experts´ Estimates at Security Risks Evaluation, In. Almanac of 8th Year of Conference: Internet and Organisational Security, University of Tomáš Baťa in Zlín, 2006, ISBN 80-7318-393-5.
[10] PECKOVÁ, Ľ: Subjects of Criminality Prevention Realization in the Slovak republic, Their Focus and Preventive Activities. Almanac of Thesis, VI. International Conference. Academy of Security and Basics of Health. Kiev 2007.

Lubomíra Pecková[1]

Crime prevention Strategy in the Slovak Republic

The Government of the Slovak Republic approved the national Crime Prevention Strategy. The implementation of this Prevention Strategy has brought a positive shift in ensuring crime prevention in particular with respect to the following aspects.

Crime prevention strategy consists of three basic parts. The first part consists of basic terms, principles and the organisations of crime prevention. It is the general part of the document. The second part contains information about the current systems in place and the state of the central body of crime prevention. The third part includes appendices like documents of the Council of Europe, United Nations Organisations, and the prognosis of the development of crime in the Slovak Republic.

The coordinating **prevention bodies** have been established at various levels:
- at a national level – The State Council for Crime Prevention of the Slovak Republic (hereinafter referred to as "Council for Prevention"),
- at the level of 12 selected ministries – crime prevention divisions (in fact divisions with cumulated functions),
- at the level of local state administration (regional authorities and district offices) – commissions for the prevention of antisocial activities (hereinafter referred to as "district and regional prevention commissions"),
- at a local level (in particular, regional and district centres) - commissions for the prevention of antisocial activities (hereinafter referred to as "local prevention commissions").

The main responsibility of prevention bodies at all levels consisted of performing tasks in the field of prevention set out on the basis of the Prevention Strategy, coordinating preparation, implementation and evaluation of preventive activities within their scope of authority, and involving the relevant entities into this process on the principle of partnership.

The functions of prevention coordinators as practitioners in particular areas have been established. Prevention coordinators are trained for their work through a specialised training programme – the basic training course conducted by the Institute for Public Administration (128 hours), under the auspices of the Council for Prevention, which also arranged the publication of the necessary study materials for the participants of the training course.

---

[1] MSc. Lubomíra Pecková, Department of Security Management, Faculty of Special Engineering, University of Žilina, Street 1.mája 32, 010 26 Žilina, Slovak Republic, tel.+ 421 513 6661, e-mail: Lubomira.Peckova@fsi.uniza.sk

At all the levels, where the prevention bodies and prevention coordinators existed and functioned, the tasks of the Prevention Strategy were developed and tailored to their own conditions in the form of prevention plans and programmes. Priorities for particular years were set out. Task performance was discussed with the prevention bodies. Special attention was paid to the prevention programmes of regional and district centres.

International cooperation in the field of prevention was provided through an expert group of the Council for Crime Prevention.

Contents of the document:
Introduction
1. Theoretical and practical background to Crime Prevention Strategy
2. Prevention system in the Slovak Republic
3. Main tasks of the Council for Crime Prevention
4. Main tasks of the central government bodies
5. Main tasks of regional authorities
6. Main tasks of regional centres
7. Annexes
8. Resolution of the Government of the Slovak Republic

1. Theoretical and practical background of prevention strategy

1.1. Terms in Prevention Strategy
(this part consists of the main definitions and classifications of crime prevention:

- **crime prevention**
- **criminality prevention**
- **crime repression**
- **crime control**
- **criminal law and other legal measures**:

The definition of target subjects represents a basis of **prevention classification** defining social prevention, situational prevention and victimisation prevention:
According to the **criterion of a crime problem development, the social** prevention, situational prevention and victimisation prevention may be implemented as:
- Primary prevention
- Secondary prevention
- Tertiary prevention

1.2. Principles of prevention

Prevention strategy will be implemented in compliance with the following principles:

1. **Principle of constitutionality and legality of prevention**
2. **Principle of the unity of repression and prevention**
3. **Principle of the scientific approach to prevention**
4. **Principle of the comprehensiveness of prevention**
5. **Principle of prevention coordination.**
6. **Principle of institutional and personnel coverage and technical equipment of prevention and professionalisation of prevention**
7. **Principle of active community involvement in prevention**
8. **Principle of financial coverage of prevention**
9. **Principle of information coverage of prevention**
10. **Principle of international cooperation in prevention**

1.3. Objectives and means of prevention

The primary objective of the implementation of preventive actions is to **promote** to the largest possible extent the **reduction of the scope and seriousness of criminal and other anti-social activities, and subsequently to reach an improvement in our citizens' feeling of safety and** reduce their fear of the threat of crime, **and thus contribute to improving the quality of life of citizens,** communities and society as a whole.

1.4. Focus of prevention

Our focus on prevention at all levels will **come from the following sources of information**:

1. analysis of development so far and the current situation, structure and dynamics of crime and other antisocial activities;
2. evaluation of crime as perceived by citizens (surveys focused on feelings of safety or threat of crime, respectively);
3. social demographic analysis;
4. prognosis of the development of crime and other antisocial activities;
5. public opinion polls;
6. experience from implementation and evaluation of the prevention activities carried out.

1.5. Forms and methods of practical implementation of prevention

Preventive activities may be carried out in different ways depending on the goal, target subject, implementer, his available resources and experience, etc. The forms and methods of prevention below are not of a normative character, however they should be considered as suggestions to be creatively applied in practice.

1.6. Evaluation of prevention

Individual preventive measures and also comprehensive prevention programmes will be subjected to a continuous and final evaluation.

2. System of crime prevention in the Slovak Republic

2.1. Levels of prevention implementation
In the Slovak Republic **a three-level system of crime prevention** has been formed, consisting of:
1. national level,
2. regional level,
3. local level.

At the national level the following tasks are performed: legislative, conceptual, economic, coordinating and executive.

At **the regional level** the following tasks are given priority:
   a) conceptual and programme tasks,
   b) coordination,
   c) economic tasks,
   d) executive.

At the **local level** tasks equivalent to those at regional level are performed, and these are modified with regard to the scope and conditions of cities, municipalities, municipal districts etc.

At all three levels:
   a) coordinating bodies of prevention;
   b) executive prevention units;
   c) financial resources to support prevention are allocated.

At all three levels the **prevention agencies** exist and function. They are the implementers of prevention activities.

2.2. Coordinating bodies of prevention

2.2.1. National level
State Council for Crime Prevention in the Slovak Republic is the coordinating body at a national level. It is an advisory, planning and coordinating government agency in the field of prevention.

2.2.2. Regional level
Coordinating prevention bodies at a regional level include:
   a) **Regional Commission for the prevention of antisocial activities.**
It is an advisory, initiative-making and coordinating body of the management of the Regional Authority and of the management of the self-governing region;
   b) **District Commission for the prevention of antisocial activities**
It is an advisory, initiative-making and coordinating body of the management of the District Office.

2.2.3. Local level

At the local level the coordinating bodies are represented by the **Town or Municipal Commissions for the prevention of antisocial activities**. They are advisory, initiative-making and coordinating bodies to the Mayor of a town or municipality.

2.3. Executive prevention units at a national, regional and the local level.

a) National level

The Secretariat of the Council is an executive unit at the Council for Prevention, which is an organisational unit in the Cabinet of the Minister of Interior of the Slovak Republic.

b) Regional level

At regional and district commissions for the prevention of antisocial activities, the executive units of prevention are represented by **prevention coordinators** integrated in an office of the relevant statutory body.

c) Local level

The executive prevention units at towns and municipality commissions for the prevention of antisocial activities are represented by **prevention coordinators** integrated in metropolitan authorities, town and community authorities.

2.4. Financial coverage of prevention

The main resource of funds for the implementation of prevention **at all levels** shall be the resources of the competent prevention bodies and agencies. **A supplementary resource** shall be provided in the form of grants, donations etc.

2.5. Legislative coverage of prevention

A bill on the prevention of crime and other antisocial activities will be drawn up in order to establish a general obligation of state authorities, self-governing bodies, the Police Force and other entities to cover prevention and related tasks. The legislative study should take place in 2008.

2.6. Research on prevention and transmission of information

It is necessary to build up a prevention information system and establish scientific research in the field of prevention. Because of this the Council for Prevention shall initiate a proposal on how to ensure the implementation of the following tasks, in particular using the capacities of the Police Academy.

2.7. International cooperation in prevention

This international cooperation will be carried out in particular in the following areas:

- Tasks with regards to the United Nations
- Tasks with regards to European institutions
- Bilateral cooperation

3. Main tasks of the council on crime prevention

This part consists of the 12 main tasks of the council on crime prevention.

4. Main tasks of Central State authorities

Ministry of Interior of the Slovak Republic
A. Police Force
B. Section of Public Administration
C. Office of Civil Protection of the Ministry of Interior of the Slovak Republic
D. Fire Brigade and Rescue Squad
E. Migration Office of the Ministry of Interior of the Slovak Republic

Ministry of Justice of the Slovak Republic
Ministry of Labour, Social Affairs and Family of the Slovak Republic
Ministry of Health of the Slovak Republic
Ministry of Education of the Slovak Republic
Ministry of Culture of the Slovak Republic
Ministry of Defence of the Slovak Republic
Ministry of Economy of the Slovak Republic
Ministry of Agriculture of the Slovak Republic
Ministry of Construction and Regional Development of the Slovak Republic
Ministry of Transport, Postal Services and Telecommunications of the Slovak Republic
Ministry of Environment of the Slovak Republic

Joint task of the central bodies of state administration:
To implement measures in order to prevent the leakage of information of classified materials.

5. Main tasks of Regional Authorities
In *Bratislava, Trnava, Trenčín, Nitra, Žilina, Banská Bystrica, Prešov, and Košice.*

6. Main tasks of regional centres

Capital City - Bratislava
Regional centre – city of Trnava
Regional centre – city of Trenčín
Regional centre – city of Nitra
Regional centre – city of Žilina
Regional centre – city of Banská Bystrica
Regional centre – city of Prešov
Regional centre – city of Košice

7. Annexes

This part consists of:
The Vienna declaration on crime and justice: Meeting the challenges of the 21st century

GUIDELINES FOR THE PREVENTION OF CRIME

8. Resolution of the government of the Slovak Republic

Conclusion

Crime prevention is not adapting in Slovak Republic law. It is still in the phase of legislative preparation and is still being considered by the Government of the Slovak Republic. It has to be passed as a law in a programmed proclamation. The law is expected to pass in 2010. The partial solution revolves around the Crime Prevention Strategy in the Slovak Republic. It aims to aid crime prevention for several years in advance. The next Crime Prevention Strategy will assist crime prevention for the period of 2007 – 2010 and it will be established in July 2007. The content of this Crime Prevention Strategy was drawn up at the 2nd International Conference on Youth Crime in Nitra, on 25-27th October 2006.

Bibliography

[1] Stratégia prevencie kriminality Slovenskej republiky (aktualizovaná na roky 2003 - 2006)
[2] BOC, K.: Plnenie úloh vyplývajúcich zo Stratégie prevencie kriminality v Slovenskej republike pre ozbrojené sily. Zborník z odbornej konferencie Prevencia kriminality a ozbrojené sily SR – model 2010. Trenčín 2002.
[3] GAŠPIERIK,L.: Prevencia kriminality. (Vybrané prednášky z prevencie kriminality pre študentov bezpečnostného manažmentu. Žilina: ŽU. Žilina,2003.
[4] Veľas, A.: Možnosti v rozvoji bezpečnosti na miestnej úrovni. In: Věda a krizové situace. Sborník přednášek. Ostrava: VŠB – TU, 8.11.2005. ISBN 80-248-0944-3.

Angelos Giannakopoulos, Konstadinos Maras and Dirk Tänzler[1]

Research Findings on Perceptions of Corruption in Seven European Countries within the EU-Project 'Crime and Culture'[2]

Brief information about the EU-Project 'Crime and Culture'

'Crime and Culture' is a specific targeted research project supported within the Sixth Framework Programme of the European Commission and coordinated at Konstanz University, Germany. It brings together 35 researchers across ten institutions in eight European countries. The research project aims to develop means to optimise corruption prevention in the EU. The urgency of such a project is reflected in the fact that corruption holds the potential to seriously hold back the process of the Community's enlargement and integration, even to the extent of threatening the very core of its concept of social order. The prevention policies that have been developed by the EU and implemented so far within individual member countries have, in general, been characterised by legislative, administrative and police force measures. These are based on a definition of corruption prevention developed in political and administrative institutions that rely on a 'top-down' procedure for its implementation. The research project pur-

---

[1] **The authors: Dr. Angelos Giannakopoulos**, Research and Teaching Associate, Department of Sociology of the University of Konstanz, Germany. Ph.D. in Sociology, University of Tübingen and Master in Political Science, University of Athens, Head of the Project Office of the research project 'Crime and Culture', Visiting Lecturer at the Eötvös Lorand University of Budapest, Hungary (2004) and Galatasaray University, Istanbul, Turkey (2007), Visiting Scholar at the Center for International and Area Studies at Yale University, USA (2004), Fellow of the Japanese Society for the Promotion of Science (JSPS) and Visiting Scholar at Waseda University, Tokyo, Japan (2007). Fields of research and teaching: modernisation of South-Eastern Europe, social history of Greece, Eastern churches' tradition and modernity, European integration and identity, cultural aspects of corruption, qualitative methods of social research.
Dr. Dr. Konstadinos Maras is Lecturer at the University of Tübingen, Faculty of Cultural Sciences, Institute of Art History and research assistant at the "European Centre for Scientific, Ecumenical and Cultural Co-operation", Würzburg, responsible for documentation and research on the European and International Philhellenism. His special research and teaching interests are Critical Theory, Aesthetics and the History of American Art, European Identity and Integration. He takes part in the EU-funded research Programme, 'Crime and Culture' as methods manager supervising the deployment of the qualitative, computer-supported content and data analysis.
Dr. Dirk Tänzler is currently visiting Professor at the University of Zurich 2007, Assistant Professor at the University of Konstanz and Co-ordinator of the EU-Research-Consortium 'Crime and Culture' 2006-2008. He was Visiting Professor at Vienna University 2005, 2006, Visiting Lecturer at the University of Luzern 2005-2008, Zeppelin University, Friedrichshafen 2006, University of Salzburg 2005, Humboldt University of Berlin 1995, 1996. Director of the Sozialwissenschaftliches Archiv Konstanz ("Alfred-Schütz-Gedächtnis-Archiv)/ Zentralarchiv der Deutschen Gesellschaft für Soziologie 2000-2005, Research Fellow at the University of Konstanz 1999-2000, Research Fellow at the Science Centre Berlin for Social Research (WZB) 1993-1997, Research Fellow at the Institute for Economic Culture at Boston University 1991-1992. He earned his postdoctoral degree (Habilitation) at the University of Konstanz 2005 and his Ph.D. at J.-W. Goethe University of Frankfurt a.M. 1990. His special research and teaching interests are Sociological Theory, Social Philosophy, History of Sociology, Sociology of Knowledge, Sociology of Culture, Political Sociology, Qualitative Methods, Hermeneutics, Media Analysis, Visual Sociology.

[2] For detailed information about the research project, research results and other important material please visit the project web site at: www.uni-konstanz.de/crimeandculture/index.htm, email: crimeandculture@uni-konstanz.de

ports to conduct not an inquiry into the nature of corruption 'as such', but rather into the perceptions of corruption held by political and administrative decision-makers in specific regions and cultures, those held by players representing various institutions and authorities, and above all by the citizens and the media in European societies. The project proceeds from the assumption that the considerably varying perceptions of corruption, determined as they are by 'cultural dispositions', have significant influence on a country's respective awareness of the problem and thereby on the success of any preventative measures. For this reason, the project investigates the 'fit' between 'institutionalised' prevention policies and how these are perceived in 'daily practice', as well as how EU-candidate and member countries as a result, handle the issue of corruption. In a final step, the research project intends to make specific recommendations for readjusting this 'fit' in the frame of an interactive scholars-experts conference in Brussels.

The members of the project consortium are: University of Konstanz (Germany, Coordinator), University of Tübingen (Germany), Police University (Federal German State of Baden-Württemberg, affiliated), Centre for Liberal Strategies (Sofia, Bulgaria), Research Institute for Quality of Life-Romanian Academy (Bucharest, Romania), Galatasaray University (Istanbul, Turkey), University of Zagreb (Croatia), National School of Public Administration and Local Government (Athens, Greece), Panteion University (Athens, Greece), South East European Studies at Oxford (United Kingdom), Centre for Research and Policy Making (FYR Macedonia, affiliated).

Cultures of Corruption and the Objectives of the Project

The goal of the research project is to deepen the knowledge of the phenomenon of corruption in the countries designated above. In doing so, it follows a twofold line of inquiry:

- The objects of the project are both the *conceptual preconditions* of the expert systems as well as the *socio-cultural conditions* under which these systems are put into effect. The project's first and second empirical phases focus on the reconstruction of the cultural patterns underlying the perceptions of corruption among players in the following target groups: Politics, Judiciary, Police, Media, Civil Society and Economy.
- Expert systems have been evaluated during the project's first empirical phase by means of a sociological analysis of documents. The field work started in the second phase by conducting interviews with persons active in all six target groups, who are involved in efforts to prevent corruption. Through the analysis of the data generated in this fashion, the common-sense definitions of corruption that hold in the respective countries will be reconstructed.
- In the third empirical phase, 'bottom-up' strategies for the prevention of corruption are to be developed on the basis of the empirical findings from phases one and two. These will serve as supplements intended to improve the effectiveness of the existing expert systems, which are presently limited to a 'top-down' approach. The existing prevention policies and procedures within the given society ('expert systems') will be submitted to a systematic strength-weakness analysis.

- On the basis of the findings from phases one to three, points of departure will be delineated for the revision of the existing expert systems. In the project's concluding phase, these will be discussed, together with policy-makers within the framework of a scholars-experts conference in Brussels and then applied to the design of new preventative policies.
- Via contacts between the project consortium, anti-corruption initiatives in the public sphere and the media, the 'common-sense perceptions of corruption', reconstructed in the first three phases, are to be communicated to the interested public. On the basis of the discussion of this concrete issue, the project will foster the development of civil-societal culture in the participating countries.

Methodically, the empirical research is designed as a content analysis following Anselm Strauss' concept of the Grounded Theory. Content analyses not only the manifest content of the material – the concept of content can be divided into:
- Themes and main ideas of the text as primary content
- Context information as a latent context. This second, non-explicit level of content analysis is all the more important since the project aims to illuminate a) the conceptual preconditions sustaining the perceptions of corruption among institutional players and b) the cultural patterns underlying both the anti-corruption policies and the understanding of corruption among the groups targeted by the prevention measures.

These two levels of the content analysis approach are interconnected by making specific inferences from the manifest content of corruption discourses to their inherent properties, that is to say motivational resources, cultural beliefs, reality assumptions and ethical values. For the purposes of the project, content analysis means fitting the research materials into a model of communication: It should be determined on what part of the communication inferences shall be made to the aspects of the communicator (experiences, beliefs, dispositions), to the situation of discourse production, to the socio-cultural underpinnings. In doing so the project neither puts any hypotheses to test nor does it validate or justify a pre-existing theory, but rather looks for a theoretical set (patterns of argumentation or schemes of reasoning) that accounts for the research situation – in our case societal perceptions of corruption – as it is. Like the Grounded Theory which supports it, the content analysis progresses inductively: The intended theoretical insights will be revealed developed and tentatively verified.

It is obvious that in this scheme the hermeneutical circle holds true in the case of content analysis. This means that unlike sampling done in quantitative investigations, theoretical sampling cannot be planned before embarking on a Grounded Theory study. The specific sampling decisions emerge during the research process itself. This in turn can only be established through the analysis of the data and the development of the ordering codes and categories. Those codes/categories are saturated when no additional data can be found that can provides further properties. In other words no further data could be supplied that functions as instances and even falsifications of these categories. Theoretical sampling comes down in practical terms to two sampling events: An initial case is selected and, on the basis of the data analysis pertaining to the case and hence the emergent theory, additional cases are selected.

This selection could be carried out either by choosing a case a) to extend the emergent theory, b) to test it or c) to supply contradictory outcomes (but for predictable reasons). As far as the collection of data is concerned, the Grounded Theory approach favours the use of multiple sources converging on the same phenomenon. Data bases from different sources widen the scope of property findings for the categories. As we are dealing with six target groups/data bases this diversity criterion has easily been matched in the project. Ordering the data in turn depends on the number of cases to be evaluated – for our project a chronological order for example does not seem to make much sense at first.

Aspects of Empirical Research Method: Codes/Categories Development[3]

- Since content analysis boils down to systematic text interpretation, it strongly depends on a reliable technique for compressing the propositions of the text into few content categories based on an explicit rule of coding. Concerning this rule, the most important guideline consists in making inferences based on the identification of core characteristics of the propositional content of the text. For their part these characteristics provide the basis for forming the codes and their interrelationships (categories).
- In the framework of the qualitative content analysis, the interpreting categories are as near as possible to the materials gathered. This means that for the most part we proceed inductively – and develop the interpretation aspects step by step, abstracting them from the textual database. Broadly speaking, formulating codes comes down to finding general variables that the propositions or a cluster of propositions in the analysed text are instances of.
- In contrast to an a priori coding that establishes the categories prior to the analysis, based upon certain theoretical presuppositions, a coding method has been chosen that relies itself on the emergent meaningfulness of certain propositions. The emerging coding is an open process in that the exploration of the relevant data is not sustained by prior assumptions of what might be discovered. This is all the more important in view of the fact that neither the data choice nor the pro-positional utterances of the players should be prejudiced. Because there was no articulated problem in advance, the research relies on generating problem cases all along the research process.
- The identification of characteristic features, as well as the inferential abstraction are especially suitable to generate recurrent patterns of argumentation and schemes of reasoning. With a certain interpretative skill they can be reconstructed on the basis of the inductive references established by the codes or categories.

---

[3] The 'ATLAS.ti' qualitative data analysis software package that is used in the consortium, supports (but does not replace) the interpretation process, for it helps considerably to reduce the volume of the pro-positional content of the texts under examination. There are two models of data analysis within 'ATLAS.ti': firstly the 'textual level' that focuses on the raw data and comprises procedures like text segmentation, coding and memo writing; and secondly the 'conceptual level' which concentrates on framework building activities such as interrelating codes, concepts and categories to form theoretical networks.

Perceptions of Corruption: Research Findings by Each Country Study Group (First Research Phase of the Project)[4]

The projects started in the first research phase with an analysis of documents from the six target groups (see above). The aim was to generate objective, i.e. manifest in documents (not 'objectively true') data of the institutional framework and the specific rationality of the field of action ('professional habit') in contrast to the subjective intentions of individual players that are explored on the basis of expert interviews from the six target groups. A leading assumption of the project's approach lies in differentiating the general institutional function a player has to fulfil, from the specific subjective perspective, in which these functional imperatives must be translated by the player under concrete action contexts.

Access to the documents was considerably more difficult than the consortium has planned. Regarding data generation, most problems were encountered in the target groups Police and Judiciary not only in EU-accession and candidate countries but also in EU-member states. Although in EU-accession and candidate countries regulations on public access to information are legally in force, the implementation there is still lacking, whereas in the EU-member states legal restrictions such as fiscal secret exist. These deficiencies had to be compensated by drawing upon supplementary material that was very informative and suitable to our research purposes despite not being specific to the cases under study.

With regard to the research process, the document analysis carried out in the first project phase has a twofold function. The document analysis provides us with first insights on the field and helps to generate issue sensibility. On this basis concrete questions for the expert interviews in the second phase have been developed.

1. Corruption in Bulgaria[5]

Perceptions of Corruption

Target Group Politics

No single definition of corruption exists amongst politicians despite the manifested consensus that corruption is a negative phenomenon that has to be combated. It appears that in the

---

[4] The presentation of project findings within this chapter is based on the executive summary on the first research phase of the project submitted by all partners of the consortium to the European Commission, DG Research. Within this chapter is there lacks specific information regarding case studies, data generation, applied methods and empirical research proceedings by each country study group, since research methodology and empirical methods described above apply to all country study groups. Accordingly, only a short description of project findings and tentative conclusions will be presented.

[5] The members of the Bulgarian study group are: Dr. Daniel Smilov (coordinator), Rashko Dorosiev (M.A.), and the research assistants Ms. Yana Papazova (M.A.) and Ms. Anna Ganeva (M.A.).

framework of privatisation, corruption could be understood in different ways depending on the current positions of the politicians and their political parties. Largely, when in power, politicians tend to praise *political privatisation* where the decisions are made on the basis of political arguments, by elected bodies having extensive powers to decide not only on the economic and formal parameters of the privatisation offers but also on a number of other issues, such as possible consequences for society as whole. On the other hand, opposition politicians claim that *political privatisation* is corrupt and favour the practice of *technical/expert privatisation*, based on purely technical and formal considerations, where appointed bodies (of independent experts) take the most important decisions following a strict legal procedure. This dichotomy is the main result of the public interest trap. The public insists on fair, but also on effective privatisation. Governments of transition countries have rapidly come to the conclusion that a fair and transparent privatisation process does not automatically produce the best outcome in terms of public interest. This is the reason why politicians while in power tend to shift the focus in defining corruption from the fairness of the process, to the quality of the results, produced in terms of the broadly defined 'public' or 'national' interest. In terms of the dichotomies described above, opposition politicians stick to public-interest bases, inclusive and inflated conceptions of corruption, which go much beyond the strict legalistic meaning of the concept. Such conceptions often allege various forms of favouritism in privatisation, clandestine state control or tacit state approval of smuggling channels; turning the party into a corrupt hierarchical structure, etc. Governing politicians usually resort to two strategies to counter corruption allegations. First, they stick to legalistic notions of corruption and require proof beyond reasonable doubt for the substantiation of corruption allegations. Secondly, and much less often, governing politicians may try to "normalise" certain practices, which the opposition calls corrupt. An extremely interesting case of this kind occurred in Bulgaria, when one of the mainstream parties attempted to sell to the public the so-called model of "circles of firms", according to which political parties have the right to build circles of friendly firms, which in turn help for the funding of the patron party. Curiously, this model was advocated as a cure against "oligarchy".

Target Group Judiciary

Not surprisingly, the target group of the judiciary resorts mainly to legalistic conceptions of corruption, and sticks to concepts and definitions in the law books. The paradoxical result of this usage is the virtual disappearance of corruption from the discourse of magistrates. In both of our case studies, the issue of corruption was renamed and translated into other problems at the judicial level. Thus, in the party funding case study, the lawsuits were about libel, and in some of these cases, the people who alleged the existence of corruption were found to violate the existing libel rules. In the privatisation case study, the problem of corruption was translated mainly into a problem of procedural violation of the privatisation law.

In both cases, what stood out was the inconclusive character of judicial proceedings as regarding the major questions at stake in the two scandals. In the party funding case, for instance, judicial proceedings could not prove or disprove the two competing interpretations of events:

the acceptance of illegal donation vs. an attempt by a controversial businessman to set up one of the major parties in the country. The unfortunate lack of conclusive judicial findings and decisions creates a fertile atmosphere for the production of myths.

Target Group Police and Prosecutors

In contrast to the judges, prosecutors and the police are characterised by a very widespread use (including in official documents) of "inflated" public interest based conceptions of corruption, such as "circles of friends", favouritism, party machines, "political umbrella against investigation", massive theft through privatisation, etc. Naming people as part of mafia-like structures – including ministers, and calculations of the negative financial impact of corrupt privatisation feature regularly in the parlance and the documents produced by this target group. Regrettably, as it became clear from the previous section, formal indictments quite rarely are upheld by courts, which creates a significant gap between the discourse and the output (sentences) of the police and the prosecutors. Our main conclusion was that this is a sign of the "politicisation" of the police and prosecutors. This means that in terms of conception and perception of corruption this group is closer to the politicians than to the judges.

Target Group Media

For the media, corruption is an all-embracing metaphor for criminal and bad government. Here, public-interest based conceptions of corruption are encountered in their most inflated versions. The main theme is that greedy and incompetent elites are stealing from the people on a massive scale. Concrete cases are usually blown out of proportion in order to paint pictures of epic theft. As a result, the borderline between investigative journalism, analysis and story-telling is often blurred and sometimes non-existent. The solutions that the media see to the problem of corruption are, as a rule, repressive in their character: more convictions. Curiously, however, sometimes the media elaborate rather daring responses to corruption, by, for instance, advancing what can be called "participatory ideals of corruption". According to these ideals, people should share in the spoils of corruption.

Such curious ideas, which find their place in the public sphere, suggest that the real role of the media is not so much in the "fight" against corruption, but rather in informing the public of latest developments in the story of grand theft. Even a cynic might say that the role of the media is in "involving" the people in these clandestine processes, making them privy to their intricacies, hooking them in the affair as a whole, albeit by means of vicarious participation. From this point of view, it is not surprising that the media, as a rule, show a disproportionate interest in the outbreak and unfolding of scandals, compared with its resolution.

Target Group Civil Society

This is by far the most sophisticated discourse about corruption, dictating the fashion in general. The main elements of this discourse are the following: corruption is measurable; it is increasing or at least is very high; it is bad for the economy. Civil society groups stress the importance of institutional change, and changes in the incentive structure of important players in the fight against corruption. Yet, and somewhat paradoxically, although they frame the solutions in terms of substantial structural reforms, results are often supposed to be expected relatively fast. This feature of civil society discourse raises public expectations dramatically. One of the results of these raised expectations is the dissatisfaction with politicians, delegitimisation of governments, and the creation of a fertile ground for the emergence of new populist political actors.

Target Group Economy

Business speaks about corruption through the discourse of silence. It prefers to shift the problem from corruption per se to the conditions for the emergence of corruption. These are usually to be found in the domain of public legislation and administration. Extremely popular is the so called problem of "red tape" – administrative hurdles for entrepreneurial activities, which are to be overcome by corrupt transactions. Generally, business discourses on corruption are depersonalised: They refer to structural conditions, not to agents and perpetrators. Business as a rule is also portrayed as the victim of corruption, while the public servants (as an anonymous category) are the potential wrongdoers. Although the conception of corruption as "grease" for the economy has been rejected by important players such as the World Bank Institute, there is no evidence that the business community has ceased to believe in this conception: On the contrary, the whole underlying structure of its perception of the problem seems to reinforce the "grease" theory. Ultimately, it could be said that there is quite a sizable disparity between the discourse of the media and the politicians, on the one hand, and the discourse of the business community on the other.

2. Corruption in Romania[6]

Perceptions of Corruption

The analysis of perceptions towards corruption of the various target groups allowed for the generation of an explorative, substantive-level theory of corruption, which consists in highlighting the definitions, characteristics and causes as well as effects of corruption.

Corruption was *defined* by all target groups in a legal/conventional manner as illegal conduct but also as altered behaviour in society, especially by NGO's. This type of definition thus expanded beyond those legally assigned. In regard to the moral grounds and values that moti-

---

[6] The members of the Romanian study group are: Prof. Dr. Ioan Marginean (coordinator), Dr. Iuliana Precupetu and the research assistants Ms. Cosmina Chitu (M.A.) and Ms. Adriana Baboi (M.A.).

vate corruption, the phenomenon is perceived as representing a breach in basic social values, based on double standards, interventions and bargaining.

Looking at the *characteristics* of corruption, there is broad agreement among the target groups that the phenomenon became generalised in all spheres of Romanian society. It is perceived as a complex mechanism, involving a subjective agreement cemented by trust. One mechanism was pointed out a number of times by several target groups: Perceptions of widespread corruption contribute to reinforcing the phenomenon, creating a snowball effect. These perceptions, which are mainly the result of the exaggerated emphasis on corruption in the media, fortify the phenomenon as people began to conceive it as a necessary condition for getting by or they are reinforced in their beliefs. At an individual level, it results in petty corruption. But it also strengthens the phenomenon in all sorts of transactions and affects various levels of society, touching the very image of the country abroad.

Most *causes of corruption* are grounded in the structural conditions of Romania and mainly in relation to the transition process of this country. Systemic characteristics of economy like its inadequate structure, the deficient economic policy, poor economic environment or short term contextual factors like privatisation of state assets, are considered as important causes that trigger corruption. The field of legislation and regulations in general is characterised mainly by incomplete reform and instability along with a low capacity of the judicial system, which add to the structural factors backing up the phenomenon. The sphere of governance contributes to corruption with features like a strenuous political reform, a formal social dialogue, the existence of various networks of interests and low quality of human resources in the political realm. The social sphere also plays a part in the phenomenon through the low level of social development of the country, the flawed institutions functioning and the powerful groups of interest.

Individual causes like human nature, the impaired relationship of citizens to the society they live in, the rent seeking behaviour and ultimately mentality, influence the existence of corruption in Romania. The *consequences of corruption* are multidimensional: political, economical as well as social. The *fight against corruption* seems to be accredited by all target groups. First, it is seen as a national priority and an absolute necessity that would serve the national interest. The assessments of current fight, though, reveal some negative aspects. Many opinions point to a fight on the façade that is delayed by effort to counter corruption and the weak political will to act against it. Institutionally, the slow building of institutions with responsibilities in fighting corruption was outlined by some groups as well as the low capacity of the judiciary to act against corruption. Recently, some progress in the efforts to battle corruption was identified by some of the groups acknowledging incipient positive results of implemented measures of anti-corruption during the past years.

This substantive level theory on corruption is an explorative attempt that will be a further testing subject. Essentially, this type of explanation is an interpretation made from given perspectives researched by scholars, its nature allowing for endless elaboration and partial negation.

The theory is limited in time and a change at any level of the conditional matrix will affect the validity of theory and its relation to contemporary reality. As conceptualising is an intellectual process that extends throughout the entire course of a given research project (Strauss/Corbin 1990), the explanation will be further structured during the next phases of the research.

3. Corruption in Turkey[7]

Perceptions of Corruption

Issuing a detailed report in 2003 entitled "Investigation of Reasons and Social and Economic Scale of Corruption, and Determination of Anti-Corruption Measures in Turkey", the parliamentary Investigation Commission defined corruption in its broadest sense as "any misuse of public administration powers in such a manner to damage public and private interests". According to the commission, corruption is the indicator of a negativity and moral weakness irrespective of the way it is defined, indicates that the society has undergone degradation in general, and can happen in such various fields as the public sector, private sector, civilian-military bureaucracies, politics or media. Terms and expressions used by other target groups in the primary and background documents reviewed here indicate that the mentioned groups' perception of corruption is not far from the definition given above.

All target groups believe that corruption is widespread in Turkey and consider it an integral part and a special form of a general degradation. Corruption was described as "dirty", "ugly" and "immoral", while corruptive acts were described as a "disgrace" and "scandal". Such expressions as "honest politics" and "clean society" turn out to be the common wishes of the target groups. All target groups shared the same conclusion that the starting point of the spread of corruption is the public sector. Perceptions of these two cases throughout two different periods of time indicate that both the corruption problem and efforts to solve the problem were considered more and more important. As for the second case, all target groups including those possessing power to make reforms agreed that what was needed was a large-scale reform movement, and although not defined, a paradigm shift.

On the other hand, the target groups criticised themselves by concluding that their efforts to fight corruption proved to be insufficient. Most of the target groups admitted that they played a direct or indirect role in the increase of and/or failure to stop corruption. Suggestions made by politicians to cancel the immunity of the Members of the Parliament (although no law was passed to that effect to date) and the circulars issued by the Ministry of Justice to the courts to order them to speed up their legal proceedings can be seen from this point of view. Non-governmental organisations admitted that they hesitated to use the rights given to them by the

---

[7] The members of the Turkish study group are: Prof. Dr. Ahmet Insel (co-ordinator), Ms. Zeynep Sarlak (M.A.) and Dr. Besim Bülent Bali.

Constitution and the laws and underline the tasks and responsibilities granted to the citizens in fighting corruption. The media passed through a similar process of self-criticism, and its partial/partisan attitude against corruption was replaced with objective criticism in time. However, the media organs did not question their own trustworthiness, their own connections with politicians, and their primary role in corruptive acts. The public knows that the media moguls also run construction, energy, telecommunication, etc. companies, and their names are involved in corruptive acts from time to time. (Allegations about relationships between the media moguls and politicians are reported to the public by rival publications). The situation is similar in the police force and the business world. The police admit that their efforts to fight corruption proved insufficient from time to time; while the business world talks so frankly sometimes that it "promises" not to become involved in corruptive acts.

The dosage and direction of criticism brought against corruption appears to be directly related to the political conjuncture and the players' positions within the balance of political power. The players' discourse about corruption changes depending on their proximity to the administration or the opposition, and their position in the accusing or accused side. The approaches of the politicians and the media to the two cases support the deduction described above. The criteria required by EU, World Bank and IMF for the consideration of membership or financial support look to have made a serious positive impact on the change of the perception model of Turkey. Especially the 'ambition' experienced in 2003 and 2004 by both the public authorities and society with regard to integration with EU caused many players to adapt a more courageous discourse on certain principles (democracy, human rights, etc.). It might be commented that this general transformation caused the overall perception of corruption to change.

IMF and World Bank also visibly had a very strong impact on especially the private sector and the civil society. The mentioned segments of our target groups undisputedly admit and repeat that the criteria required by IMF, World Bank and EU to solve the corruption problem are preliminary conditions for integration with the "modern West". On the other hand, most of the target groups voice their worries over the future of the fight against corruption between the lines. This point indicates that the notion of fight against corruption has not settled in the political culture of Turkey yet.

The media, non-governmental organisations and economic agents frequently express their worry that unless permanent measures are taken, the political agenda might quickly shift to populism in the future. It is observed at this point that they emphasise that the supportive role of the EU is as important as the determination of the Turkish players. All of the target groups including the politicians admit that it is true that politics in Turkey are based on a mechanism of distribution of favours (nepotism, favouritism).

At this stage of the review no emphasis on petty corruption, which is so widespread in this country could be found, and which has turned into a kind of 'normal' practice. However, a number of colloquial expressions that spread (or were coined) in the Turkish language in the last 10 to 15 years, which are impossible to translate but can be described as variations to the English expression "riding the gravy train", do not have much negative connotation. This approach contributes to the understanding of corruption as something legal as defined above. When the value shift that took place on the individual ground thanks to the distorted, uncontrolled, unplanned liberal reform process right after the coup d'état of 1980 coincided with the existent "communitarian" and "solidarist" social values, the situation becomes even more complex. Is petty corruption perceived as a means to speed the completion of official formalities while grand corruption is perceived as wasting of the economic resources? We believe that it is important for us to focus on this question in the second part of our study.

4. Corruption in Croatia[8]

Perceptions of Corruption

The analysis suggested the existence of six distinct models of understanding of corruption in Croatia.

(1) *The Public Relations model* – simplified, populist and/or one-dimensional definition of corruption, where corruption is perceived primarily as damaging for the public image of the institution/players in question, and measures for fighting corruption are evaluated according to the PR efficiency criteria;

(2) *The Expert model* – complex and comprehensive definition of corruption; corruption is seen as damaging the socio-cultural fabric of society and economically wasteful; measures for fighting corruption are based on best international practice.

(3) *The Nuisance model* – no clear definition of corruption. It is a minor and omnipresent issue that has been overblown and measures for fighting corruption should be *ad hoc* and situation-specific.

(4) *The Human Rights model* – a comprehensive definition emphasising human rights and individual responsibility; corruption is a moral, socio-cultural and economic evil; measures for fighting corruption should be extremely rigorous, transparent and inclusive (allowing an active role of the civil society).

(5) *The Pragmatic model* – a comprehensive definition linked to legal description; corruption is a major social problem, both on individual and collective level; measures for fighting corruption need to be systematic, well coordinated and assisted by international aid.

(6) *The Ignoring model* – usually *ad hoc* and declaratory definition; corruption becomes problematic only when it severely impedes governance and where measures for fighting corruption are largely absent.

---

[8] The members of the Croatian study group are: Prof. Dr. Aleksandar Stulhofer (coordinator), Prof. Dr Ognjen Caldarovic, Prof. Dr Kresimir Kufrin and the research assistants Ms. Margareta Gregurovic (B.A.), Ms. Martina Detelic (Candidate B.A.), Mr. Ivan Landripet (B.A.), Ms. Iva Odak (Candidate B.A.) and Mr. Bojan Glavasevic (Candidate B.A.).

The models need to be seen primarily as *Weberian* ideal types and not as empirical entities. In reality, most of the proposed models can be found only in fragments or as an array of slightly different versions. Also, it would be mistaken to assume that each target group could be represented by a single model. Most target groups were characterised by several different models or, more precisely, by a number of elements taken from different models of corruption.

In a preliminary fashion, the analysis suggests specific linkages between the models and target groups. The PR (public relations) model seems to be present in the target group Politics and partially in the Legal System target group. In both target groups, the P (pragmatic) model was also found – as well as in the target groups Police and, partially, Civil Society. The N (nuisance) model seemed to be characteristic of the city government and administration (target group Politics), while the I (ignoring) model was found to be mostly associated with the target group Economy, but partially also with the Legal System. The E (expert) model seems to be present in a number of target groups, such as Civil Society (the case A), the Media (the case A), Politics (the parliamentary opposition) and partially Economy, the Legal System (the new national anti-corruption strategy) and the Police. Finally, the HR (human rights) model was also associated with Civil Society (the case B), Politics (Ombudsman's report) and the Media (the case B) target groups.

It is obvious that the conclusions are tentative at best. In some cases the number of documents collected proved insufficient for producing conclusions that could accurately reflex the complexity of approaches within a target group. In some other instances the character of documents analysed was proved as unsuitable or too ambivalent for reaching any definite conclusion. For these and other reasons, the linkages between the (ideal-typical) models and the six target groups need to be taken with great caution.

5. Corruption in Greece[9]

Perceptions of Corruption

Corruption is referred to as a *social illness* and occasionally as a *social phenomenon* and *by-product* of modern societies. Nevertheless, several texts share a strong critical view of representatives of the state. This is more intense in the media, which promote themselves as defenders of the public and guardians of public ethics. It also implies the increasing power of the media in Greek society. However, the criticism does not seem to be affecting politicians, since they continue to consider themselves the main group responsible and suitable for corruption control and promotion of transparency in society. They support new legislation, control and inspection mechanisms.

---

[9] The members of the Greek study group are: Prof. Dr. Effi Lambropoulou (coordinator), Ms. Stella Ageli (M.A.), Ms. Eleftheria Bakali (M.A.), Mr. Nikolaos Papamanolis (M.A.) and Dr. Vassilis Bourliaskos.

Public administration receives the strongest criticism, as being the basic impediment to transparency and therefore the development of the country; unlike the private economy which is presented as the main "victim" of corruption in the country. The remaining groups try for a clear role in the discourse on corruption. The Judiciary promotes more legislation, the Police more control, while the Media whatever the case may be, and the NGO's try to fit somewhere into the field. In general, the various target groups regard the issue according to their requirements, roles and interests. More specifically:

Politics: Although politicians refer several times to "merging of interests", "corruption" etc., when a specific case emerges their debates turn to be mostly party-political. Thus, the debates are focused on the denial of responsibility, referring rather to "misgovernment" than to corruption. It is interesting that politics borrows the meaning of corruption from media and the reverse. As far as the public administration is concerned, high ranking civil servants remain adherent to dominant and traditional views. Contrary to them, the (Civil Servants) Union members seem to share a more elaborated approach and tend to be more open-minded and share more original thoughts.

Justice: The courts are strictly focused on supporting their decision, with references and statements of the plaintiffs. The word corruption is non-existent in their text.

Police: The reports contain rhetoric and descriptive statements on the state and ethics. They overemphasise the effectiveness of the Service and they often stress the role of the police as "objective, impartial, and corresponding to society's needs". The use of the word *corruption* is rare. The Service focuses almost exclusively on corrupt practices of public administration.

Media: For the media corruption remains a news story valuable for its threshold and personalisation. It is considered a *social illness*, which requires the commitment of the whole society to be cured. Sometimes the discourse reverts to condemnation against the whole society.

Civil Society: NGOs analyse corruption mostly employing a well documented argumentation, still with emotional-cum-ethical statements. Thus, the issue is "a fight" and "a battle" against illegal practices and corruption.

Economy: The views of the economy as presented in its texts are one-sided, not resulting from a thorough analysis of the country's particularities. They regard "political-party interests, social class interests and complicated legislation" as the main causes of corruption.

From the research it became obvious that a channel of communication and promotion of views among different social groups operates (here: Media, NGOs, and Politics). Those social groups who do not have access to the media are an easy mark for condemnation and stigmatisation; the same applies to large and diffuse groups because it is difficult for them to defend themselves. It is interesting that according to the texts analysed, the *official perceptions* of corruption in Greece are not considerably different from the corresponding reports of international organisations (TI, OECD, World Bank, etc). Therefore, it eventually expresses the influence of those organisations, which include the ranks and scores on corruption. And it might question, as far as Greece is concerned, whether a "bottom-up" approach to corruption would bring some different results to the "top-down" process. Since citizens' views are not included, our findings cannot yet support the results of other research that the followed behaviour (everyday behaviour) does not necessarily coincide with legitimation of corruption or that moral disapproval of corruption necessarily associates with willingness to make a complaint about it. Otherwise, how can the low score of Greece in the CPI's index be explained?

6. Corruption in Germany[10]

Perceptions of Corruption

Target Group Politics

In the context of parliamentary debates on the illegal party financing that the ex-chancellor and leading party officials of the Christian Democratic Party were involved in and bearing in mind that at the same time, the bribes that leading party officials of the Social Democratic party in Cologne received, the main standpoint that underpins the perceptions and arguments of the political players is one of *mutual discredit and delegitimation*. The main political formations outbid each other, continuously raising the claim that the opponent, being himself morally disqualified or lacking the integrity, has no legitimate right to castigate the wrongdoings of the other side [double-bind]. The parliamentary inquiry committee is perceived as a continuation of *party struggle with other means*. Resolute transparency undermines the very fundaments of a *fair party competition,* exposing the financial transactions to the gaze of the political enemy eager to draw advantages. The illegal donations of the Kohl era further raise the question of whether the whole affair should be subsumed under the notion of *political corruption*. Taking into account the definition of TI, it is far from clear that the 'system' of secret accounts testifies beyond doubt to the fact of *politically corrupt conduct*. The reason for this lies both in the fact that a) *no private benefits* were intended or factually gained, and b) no sufficient evidence could be delivered that *receiving the donations was causally connected to the political decision process. Political corruptio*n understood as a *distortion of party democracy* can however be observed – it did not occur between donors and politicians, but rather as a means to keep the party organism under the authoritarian rule of Kohl. By means of this authoritarianism Kohl *reversed the priorities* of the ethical conduct preferring to uphold the private ethic of the 'word of honour' against the law-conforming ethic of public accountability. The case ended in that indeterminate area between sanctionable corruption and general political exercise of influence.

The corruption scandal in Cologne involving party officials of the Social Democratic Party (SPD) who received bribes after the deal to build a garbage incinerator was struck, essentially revolves around the violation of the rules of open and public procurement procedures. Circumventing existing regulations in the field was perceived by the local authorities in the state

---

[10] The members of the German study group are: Prof. Dr. Dirk Tänzler (coordinator), Dr. Dr. Konstadinos Maras, Dr. Angelos Giannakopoulos and the research assistant Ms. Bettina Grimmer (M.A. cand.).

of North Rhine-Westphalia as unavoidable since they a) *relied* on the economic efficiency the technical know-how of the construction companies guaranteed and b) *were keen on* securing a considerable number of jobs in the region. Additionally blame is put on the funding and finance management of the party allowing the *transformation* of 'sweeteners' into financial contributions. Certain parallels are also drawn to the 'Kohl system' in that the local officials of the SPD, once monetarily gratified for their decision, used the bribes to foster political career planning – in the face of the neo-liberal reforms of the public sector deploying private-public partnerships, this is perceived as inevitable. In this way a certain view of the whole affair can even assume the character of a *fatalist acquiescence* to the inevitability of corrupt conduct on the part of individuals that are considered to be prone to 'deviant behaviour', as neither the party financing regulations can wipe out 'deviant' conduct nor can they ever deter those determined to pursue their interests with criminal energy. Enforcing sanctions and transparency measures must nevertheless be seen as compulsory since it puts the capacity of the political system for *self-purification* to test.

Target Group Judiciary

The analysis of the perceptual patterns of corruption by judges and lawyers is based on a court dossier on the so-called "Financial Scandal of Cologne's SPD", that happened during the project development for a residual waste incineration plant in the 1990's. The arguments and rhetoric deployed by the prosecutors and the judges is dominated by two rationalities: that of legalistic expertise, but also that of the daily experience of people or the everyday layman. Alongside the 'stylistic' expressions of the legal rhetoric one also finds a classification of diverse incidents of bribery, so to say the *semantics of corruption*.

In the Bill of Indictment and the Sentence, two lines of argument relating to perceptions and interpretation patterns of corruption stand out. On the one hand the judges develop a *description* and a *reconstruction* of acts, and issue judgements on the basis of laws, legal commentaries and sentences from 'precedent setting cases', on the other hand – in central parts of the prosecution and sentencing argument – they *make use of 'common-sense' arguments*, regularly referring to the 'real life' context. While considering the *motives for corrupt behaviour* the jurists develop a *typology of bribery* according to their findings in their investigations and witness statements. There is a distinction in the files between the 'tempting' of individual politicians and the 'political landscape conservation' of parties and factions. The so-called 'impact bribes' must be distinguished from that. These are extraordinarily high one time payments for a specific purpose, which, legally speaking, seal an 'accord of injustice', a fraudulent contract. Such 'accords of injustice' are made in secrecy and silence, meaning in collusion or as a silent agreement, without explicit discussion of the matter. "Impact donations" aim to influence a decision in the future, "thank-you donations" are less objectionable gifts for services rendered. Fundamental to a case of corruption is not whether the political decision was truly influenced by the bribe or not, but solely if the "accord of injustice" was agreed upon, be it in good or bad faith. From a legal standpoint it is important that the recipient of the donation believes that decisions will be taken in his favour; otherwise the donation would be pointless "money thrown out the window" for the giver. Any other explanation according to this argument would be a departure from "real life". The case shows that in the eyes of judges and lawyers the logic of corruption is not determined by the fact that the decision is influenced (a connection difficult to objectify), but by a corrupt contract, in the sense that expectations are tied to a payment.

Target Group Police

The reconstruction of the perceptual patterns of corruption among the criminal prosecution authorities is based on the investigation files from the Department for Special Cases of Organised Crime at the State Police Headquarters in Freiburg, in Baden-Württemberg, Germany, dealing with two cases of corruption: *a*) The first case deals with 'active bribery' in the German construction industry, an economical branch in which corruption is virtually 'common practice', *b*) the second with 'passive bribery' involving an official of the city's Immigration Office, which played a key role in a people-smuggling ring.

The perceptual patterns of corruption among the criminal prosecution authorities are shaped by the formal procedures, they are obliged to follow by law. For the officials involved corruption ("bribery") is of course legally a clearly defined fact. Nonetheless, the measures taken to *reconstruct* the crime, the *milieu* in which it occurred and the *motives* behind it in particular are highly informative for an understanding of the attitudes and the perceptions of corruption which influence the investigative process. There are certain images of the typical course of a crime, offender profiles and the criminal milieu 'in the heads of the investigating officers' which guide them in their work.
In the case of the 'gentleman's crime' in a branch of industry which is strongly marked by corruption, the motive presented in the file is not so much personal enrichment as the *pursuit of entrepreneurial success*. The economic advantages achieved by corruption would primarily serve the *consolidation and development of the 'business empire'* and the satisfaction of personal strivings for power and property would thus only be a secondary aim. This perhaps explains the social tolerance towards such practices in industry, as opposed to the reaction towards the activities of people-smugglers, obviously dealing with the illegal activities of a commercial gang motivated by the desire for *personal enrichment*. The suspected official from the Local Immigration Office reveals the 'classic' characteristics of passive corruptibility: Employment in public service with contacts to the general public, the complicated issue of legal residence, personal financial problems, precarious family situation, acceptance of small presents, invitations to dinner, travel, emotional attachment linked with material dependence and the complicity of others in his breach of duty (which places him 'in the hands of' the persons practising 'active bribery').

These images or perceptual patterns that could be reconstructed in the files are based on *professional expertise, experience* in the field, but also on social *prejudices*. Professional expertise is the dominating perspective in the phase of providing evidence for the charge. To find out the motivation for the crime reference to a broader set of knowledge and experience is usual. Then social prejudices play an eminent role.

Target Group Media

With regard to the two print media analysed, one can assume that the central pattern of corruption examined in the 'Frankfurter Allgemeine Zeitung' refers to the belief of the *self-healing* powers of the political and party system. The crisis related to the so-called 'black-accounts' of the CDU party is by no means perceived as a state crisis but at least as a leadership crisis of a single party. The 'Süddeutsche Zeitung' on the other hand rests its hopes on the rule of law, democratic order and the control of individual power to combat and prevent corruption. Its criticism goes beyond the party system in Germany even accusing the judiciary being weak against political influences.

Regarding the two TV talk shows chosen, the first one, 'Sabine Christiansen', handles the corruption issue in the manner of political expertise, whereas the second one, 'Hart aber fair', seeks to confront the case head on, often using populist arguments. In this way the objective, professional manner, in which the first talk show helps *normalise and objectify* the corruption scandals, contrasts strongly with the *moralising attitude of ethical indictment* of the second that resembles the attitude of the 'Süddeutsche Zeitung', favouring a deep mistrust of politicians, relying at the same time on institutional control and the force of civil society.

Two continuous patterns of perception of corruption are common to both the articles of the examined print media as well as the talk shows, which do not exclude each other, but rather merge into a pattern of interpretation: a) corruption as a problem of *breach of trust* in terms of human morality and *b*) corruption as a *control problem* in technical terms. These two patterns of perception by the media are related on the one hand to certain values and to technical procedures of exercising power within a democratic community on the other. Corruption is accordingly understood both as a failure of the institutionalised procedures of the political system and an expression of human weaknesses.

Target Group Civil Society

In marked contrast to the relative disinterestedness of the economic world regarding the issue of corruption, the activities of civil society organisations such as TI have contributed importantly to raise public awareness on the matter. In terms of awareness, it plays a crucial role in the reduction of inequalities or the promotion of equal chances in the party competition – the normal mechanisms of competition in the framework of market economies apparently not guaranteeing a fair play of forces –, but also in minimising the intrusion of the economic exchange logic into the political sphere, Transparency International declares party financing to be one of the most central *steering mechanisms* of lawful and transparent party work. However a certain level of caution should be observed on the issue of *balancing* input regulations and output effectiveness/supervision complying with the requirement of *proportionality* between means and results; regulatory overdrive may run counter to societal perceptions of human rights. As a supplementary rule-setting strategy to ensure the conformity of economic transactions to law (for example in cases of public procurement) the TI has launched the Integrity Pact, planned to function as a containment of 'deviant' dispositions. At the core of TI's *'bottom-up'* approach in fighting corruption lies the network of ALACs (Advocacy and Legal Advice Centres) in various countries, promoting societal initiatives from groups or individuals to articulate their complaints against what is perceived as corrupt conduct, helping them at the same time to reclaim their rights.

Target Group Economy

The analysed data from the Federation of German Trade Unions (DGB) generally demonstrates that important social and political dimensions of corrupt practices are not subject to consideration by the Federation. The perception of the DGB seems to be a rather restrictive one. The anti-corruption strategy of the DGB centres almost exclusively on the immediate risks corruption represents for the company and in particular for the workforce. This explains the significance the DGB assigns to institutionalising and implementing concrete measures for so called whistle-blowing within companies.

Though this anti-corruption strategy is common between trade unions on the one hand and employers' federations on the other, the latter firstly underline *the extent* to which corruption *distorts* ('corrupts') competition in a market economy. Especially regarding the regulations on public contracting and the establishment of a corruption register (at least at the level of the federal states in Germany), it is clear to see that *synergy effects* are developing between the activities of politicians, NGOs and the business world. If one compares the claims raised by industry and TI and addressed in politics, then one can easily observe the existence of a broad cooperation between politics, the economy and civil society aimed at fighting corruption.

However, there are two main facts that point to the assumption that combating *corruption does not belong to the high priorities* of 'labour and capital' organisations. The first one is the quantitative 'meagreness' of the documents produced by them, the second one the 'qualitative' lack of the documents. In general, the recommendations of both organisations to fight corruption within companies in principle refer to a double strategy: Improving *structures of control in the workplace* and *strengthening the sensitive business ethics* on the subject of corruption. Although the interests of capital and work are irreconcilable and their relationship tends to be conflicting, it is nevertheless obvious that corporate structures in the sense of so called 'Rhineland capitalism' on the one hand and the rhetoric of industrial ethics on the other are the very core of the frame within which labour and capital perceive corruption and anti-corruption measures in Germany. Both of them concentrate on structural and ethical measures, i.e. strengthening of controls and complementary moral elements of anti-corruption. Moreover, the corporate alliance between capital and labour is additionally flanked by a balance of interests and the process of accommodation between both civil society and the state.

Conclusions

The public debates in Germany are sustained by the belief that the country is 'clean' of corruption. Corruption at the level of every-day life is deemed negligible and institutions and public administration are seen as working properly. From the analysis of the documents undertaken, it becomes evident that primarily political corruption increases public interest. In contrast to political corruption, economic corruption is not regarded as a destabilising factor. The reason for this lies in the argument that seeking advantages and enrichment are after all part and parcel of the driving forces in economic life, but they are by no means compatible with the principles of democratic politics. The intermingling of political and economic rationale is considered as the origin of corruption in the public administration. Changes in the perceptions of corruption can be observed in Justice, Police and Public Administration. In the cases of Civil Society (except for the NGO's), Politics and Economy, the matter is less clear. One must always distinguish between public statements and actual actions.

7. Corruption in the United Kingdom[11]

Perceptions of Corruption

Amongst all target groups (but less so from the Media), a strong sentiment was evident that standards of public office are generally high in the UK. The Media tended to add their support to this view when the situation in the UK was compared regionally or globally.

A strong variation in views on corruption was evident especially within the Media and Politics target groups (unsurprisingly), and limited a variation from the NGO group and Judiciary. No variation was found in the documents from the Police target group. The constraints of their position and remit, and the source of the documents (as official sources in the case of official bodies), clearly limited the types of arguments that were put forward from the Politicians, Judiciary and Police; wide-ranging structural and cynical arguments were most likely to be made by the Media, followed by NGOs.

The area of most concern amongst all target groups was the relationship between business and politicians. The details of the concerns varied; whether the relationship was rightly or wrongly viewed with suspicion, when corruption took place which party was more likely to be the instigator (i.e. more culpable than the other), to what extent was either party sincere in its anticorruption statements or what other possible self-interest or pressures motivated them to make them.

---

[11] The members of the British study group are: Dr. Othon Anastasakis (coordinator), Dr. Sappho Xenakis and Mr. Kalin Ivanov (M.A.).

As suggested by the project's initial outline, the media was widely acknowledged as playing an important role in mobilising public opinion and thereby generating pressure in support of anti-corruption efforts. However, the media were also the subject of criticism for being perceived to be more interested in whipping up public fervour over the issue than ensuring substance to their allegations of scandal. The integrity of the media in their role as informer and stimulator of public opinion and reaction was called into question. Furthermore, it was pointed out that sometimes the media are often credited for being a more active and effective anti-corruption tool than they can legitimately claim, since their reports of investigations are often mistakenly read as the work of the media organisation itself.

NGOs were also recognised for their important role in the shaping of opinion within Parliament and amongst the public, although it was clear that amongst NGOs themselves quite different attitudes towards the issue of corruption were apparent. An interesting preliminary finding from the NGO and politicians' focus groups in the first case study concerned the perceived acceptability of a certain degree of patronage in politics and conceptions about where the ideal limits to it were to be drawn.

It was nevertheless evident that British perceptions and discourse on corruption have been undergoing a significant period of evolution since the mid 1990s, and many of these changes are still underway in the UK (including, for example, the issue of patronage in political life) and outcomes are still as yet unclear. The activism of the past decade or so has itself been described as a positive step by all but the more cynical observers (who proposed that such transformations were superficial but powerful forms of propaganda, clothing the reality of 'business as usual') that were found in the material gathered.

The under-use of the word 'corruption' in the material collected also appeared to be a significant issue on which comments were addressed within the material. The word 'corruption' tends to be avoided in the material, while and others such as 'standards in public life', 'sleaze' and 'cronyism' preferred. While these are certainly imbued with a negative imagery, 'corruption' appears to be a term associated with more severe conditions of corruption perceived to be bedevilling other countries. The paucity of documents relating to the subject or cases of corruption, amongst the target groups was the subject of analysis by far fewer (and somewhat evidently so) among the target groups. Existing in-depth academic literature on the causes of this lack of documents, was not included in the studies; this omission is likely to be remedied in the proceeding period of research.

The most significant divisions of perspective concerned prognoses for change; the more cynical views expressed considered the problems of corruption to be systemic and therefore implied that an overhaul of the political system would be necessary to alter the *Realpolitik* nature of policy and allow ethical policies to be genuinely prioritised. The majority of views expressed were more moderate; that more regulation and better enforced oversight practices would go a long way to dissuading would-be corruptors from perpetrating their crime. A minority again characterised corruption as a rare act committed by individuals; this perspective encouraged the maintenance of tradition and was clear in the business and politicians' target groups, from those seeking to maintain the contemporary limits of their autonomy and anxious not to incur greater incursions into their freedom of movement or invasion of their private business.

Some Tentative Overall Conclusions

The summary reports of the research teams' findings in the first phase of the research work do not follow a uniform presentation style. While some remain close to the case studies examined, presenting perceptions of corruption from the six target groups directly related to the cases, others favour a more abstract approach, trying to bundle up recurrences of perception in ideal-type models. This divergence can also be observed between the reports that stick to the six-fold pattern of structuring the presentation, some of them pinpointing the particular and context determined attitudes towards the corruption case involved, others seeking instead to unify the findings in overtly generalising terms resulting from subsuming the first-level codes under more abstract second-level notions purporting to go beyond the specific modalities obtained in the fields of perceptions attached to each of the target groups. These differences in presenting the findings are to some extent the result of *a*) the documents being in certain cases unsatisfactory concerning quantity – mainly in the target groups 'Police' and 'Judiciary' –, but also apparently *b*) the fact that it is sometimes problematic to extract clear-cut stances from the ways the target groups cope with or respond to phenomena of corruption can serve as a basis to establish perception patterns.

The aforementioned differences notwithstanding, it is obvious that on the basis of the content analysis of the data, certain homologies occur between the findings of the country research groups. They concern both patterns of perception, specific to each target group, and higher level notions running across the societal sectors marked by the target groups as well. Nevertheless, the level of generalisation achieved in the frame of the research work of the country groups may well capture certain *'home-grown' specificities* - perception patterns unexplainable without taking into account the background character of the national culture, but this proves in a certain sense too *narrow a basis for conclusion transfers*. Keeping this in mind it is however worth drawing some parallels concerning corruption perceptions specific to the target groups examined. Grouping them together in a comparative cross-national analysis can provide first-rate observations on how the societal rationality types represented by the six target groups correlate with specific perceptions of and attitudes towards the corruption phenomena.

Firstly turning to the target group *Politics*, such perceptions can be discerned to the extent that the ramifications of the relations between money and politics are explored. As the German and the Bulgarian cases show, the positions of the players towards the phenomena of political corruption depend essentially on *a*) whether the party they are engaged in holds political power or not (this being also the case according to the findings of the Turkish research group) and *b*) certain assumptions concerning the party's economic, i.e. financial capacities. Consid-

ering a) corrupt conduct, that means illegal party financing and/or the rule-violating deployment of party finances, is sometimes (or regularly) deemed legitimate by the political players
given the fact the achievement of certain goals of national gravity are perceived as dependent
on unavoidable law deviations. The same trait of inexorableness can be discerned in their perceptions of legitimate deviations resulting from them feeling under continuous pressure owing
to the 'structural financial blight' of their parties. This last 'menace' also extends to the opposition parties that of course do not want to falter in the party competition over funding resources. Another interesting parallel that can be established between the two country findings
concerns the relation between transparency and the equality principle. In Bulgaria perceptions
of corruption are centred round the issue of the lack of transparency that overrides the necessity of scrutinising the structural causes of corruption, originating in the disproportional influence of corporate interests in politics. In Germany the lack of transparency has sometimes
been used to buttress the argument that it is by no means detrimental to the interest equality in
terms of party competition, as it can clearly be shown for example in the party financing affair
of the former Kohl government. Regarding the latter it seems to be a common denominator of
political attitudes on corruption being made an object of party political contestation regarding
its definition and character (see also the Greek case).

The way perceptions of corruption are articulated in the **Mass Media** offers a rather complicated picture. For one thing, it is not always an easy task to define the role the mass media
play where not only cases of corruption are made public, but also allegations of corrupt conduct that are often taken at face value. The contribution of the media to societal corruption
discourses can sometimes exacerbate the gravity of the very same phenomenon they otherwise purport to expose and castigate, as the Romanian, Bulgarian and Turkish target group
studies plainly show. Aggravating the problem means that the media either jump on the
bandwagon of rigorous public indictment and populist indignation casting the whole political
class under suspicion of 'stealing' the public (Bulgaria), fortify the phenomenon by rendering
it a semi-natural occurrence that the citizens must get by or cope with as one normally does
with other natural events (Romania), or even they are themselves, i.e. the powerful owners of
the media corporations, part and parcel of wrongdoing networks (Turkey). Amplifying effects
concerning corruption being perceived as 'natural' also develop the media to the extent that
they attribute the propensities to corrupt conduct to certain human weaknesses (as shown in
the case of the German media). One must also not forget the *mediating* function the *media*
fulfil acting as a mechanism of selective problem articulation between the civil society and
the political sphere: Having access to the media means more often than not setting the stage
for corruption 'awareness' (see the Greek case).

The articulation of corruption perceptions in the *Judicial Sector* was rather difficult to elaborate in the framework of the research work carried out on the target group 'Judiciary' due to
the strict legalistic discourses dominant in the field. The problem of distilling societal perceptions from lawsuits concerning corruption cases originates form the fact that judicial players
translate, or even better, reconstruct the course of events exclusively in terms of the codified
language of law prosecution (see for example the Bulgarian and Greek case studies). Apart

from that, the findings of the research groups point out that the judicial system has in the past failed to live up to the expectations of effective corruption prosecution because of the incomplete implementation of reforms (Romania) or bureaucratic inertia (Turkey). However, depending on the quality of the documents secured by the German research group, it can be shown that the judicial discourse does not necessarily constrain the multifaceted phenomenon of corruption to its legally codified aspects (see also the English findings relating to the judiciary): Apart from the processing rules of the legalistic expertise, the arguments deployed by prosecutors and the judges sometimes observe another rationality too, namely that of tacit knowledge or situation specific characterisations of corrupt conduct. In a double layered approach, the description or/and reconstruction of the case proceeding along the lines of judicial reasoning is accompanied by 'common-sense' arguments, regularly referring to the 'real life' context (see the German case).

The corruption discourse in the target group *Police* contains elements that show a certain affinity to widespread societal notions characterising the phenomenon regarding their relevance to perceptions of corruption, to the extent that it is not limited by the formal constraints of technical-procedural expertise. The 'closeness' to socially anchored attitudes takes the form of either *a*) a reconstruction of the case guided by tacit knowledge assumptions about the milieu it occurred in and the driving motives of the players involved (see the findings in the German case), or *b*) the use of widely circulating notions and/or stereotypical formulations (see the Bulgarian case). For the most part however the police- specific attitudes to corruption want to maintain a certain degree of 'impartiality' reflecting societal interests and the general public good (see the Greek case, something similar seems to apply in the English case).

The findings relating to corruption perceptions that can be observed in the *Economic Sphere* display a greater variety. Indeed the spectrum of what the causes of corruption are or how it should be coped with effectively, ranges from attitudes that straightaway deny corruption having anything to do with the economic life thus relegating and/or 'externalising' its causes to the realm of politics on the one hand (Bulgaria, Greece), to attitudes that see the causes rooted in the realm of economy, attributing them nevertheless to the still transitional character of the reform process on the other (Romania). It can even happen that the intrinsic propensities towards corruption in the business world is frankly admitted by the players in the field who are only too ready to assure that they will refrain from wrongdoing (Turkey). The German case could somehow be situated in the middle: On the one hand both trade unions and employers' federations look up to politics as a rule-setting model, developing regulations to the effect of curbing corruption in the economic world. One the other hand an awareness of 'home-grown' causes is not lacking – strengthening control structures and the appeal to the virtues of the corporate spirit of 'Rheinischer Kapitalismus' are nevertheless deemed sufficient to keep corrupt conduct at bay.

The *Civil Society* and the *NGO*'s working in the field of anti-corruption unsurprisingly show a high level of problem awareness, especially regarding those aspects of behavioural changes concomitant with the reform process of the transition period (Romania). However, raising sensibility concerning the 'dark sides' of the reform process may not always have a positive function, for the demand for substantial changes called for by civil society players raises the level of expectations so high that, in the absence of short term improvements, the dissatisfaction with the political reform efforts leads to a delegitimisation of the political sphere, thus ushering in populist 'alternatives' (Bulgaria). Corruption is largely perceived in terms of moral categories (see the Greek and Turkish cases), that is as a moral and socio-cultural evil (according the Human Rights Model of the Croatian research group). Beyond the level of moral indictment the work of the anti-corruption NGO's – first and foremost that of TI – concentrates on setting up strategies to ensure the law conformity of economic transactions: the German TI for example has launched the Integrity Pact to be observed in public procurement procedures. Furthermore establishing the network of ALACs (Advocacy and Legal Advice Centres) TI follows a 'bottom-up' approach in fighting corruption.

Summing up, it can be observed that all reports pinpoint certain recurrences characterising societal corruption perceptions, with the Croatian report furthermore, delivering certain discursive patterns that raise the claim of covering all those societal action fields represented by the target groups under examination. It remains to be seen to what extent the analysis of the interviews to be conducted in the second research phase will lead both to perception and discourse patterns.

Wiesbaden Declaration of the 12th German Crime Prevention Congress "A strong youth – a strong future"

Since its inception in 1995 the German Congress on Crime Prevention (*DPT – Deutscher Präventionstag*) has focussed on youth crime and its prevention as one of its important and ongoing topics. The 12th Congress on Crime Prevention (held on the 18th and 19th of June in Wiesbaden) placed presentations, consultations, discussions and Dr Steffen Wiebke's expert opinion "Youth crime and its prevention - perceptions versus empirical evidence" under the heading "A strong youth – a strong future". On the basis of the aforementioned expert opinion the *DPT,* its standing partners and this year's hosting sponsors unequivocally state that:

Crime prevention works

⇒ Over the last few years there have been encouraging developments in the areas of youth crime and youth violence, not least because efforts regarding crime prevention amongst children and young people have been considerably stepped up. Preventive strategies have led to remarkable progress.

⇒ Strategies aimed at the prevention of violence are mainly dominated by pedagogical strategies inspired by the fact that the prevention of violence amongst children and young people must be linked to aspects of growing up. The DPT supports these approaches.

⇒ Violence during adolescence should be addressed in terms of everyday education, clearly defined learning, engendering self-esteem, learning to resolve conflicts without resorting to violence as well as acquiring and practising other social skills.

⇒ In this sense violent acts by children and young people constitute a challenging opportunity for those who actively pursue prevention work with the aim of teaching the young people concerned concrete and effective life experiences.

⇒ To this end it is vital to react to potentially relevant behaviour under criminal law and to set youngsters clearly defined limits. This can be achieved by means other than using criminal law. Informal reactions by parents, teachers, friends and other people to whom children and young people closely relate have proved to be very effective.

⇒ In Germany's federal *Laender* and its regions violence prevention strategies have both been accepted and established and have generally led to positive results. However, certain aspects need improving, including better targeting on certain groups such as young intensive offenders and young people with migration backgrounds. It is also extremely important to strengthen the perspective of the victims.

⇒ One of the most important challenges for the DPT is to embed, promulgate and develop existing strategies. This includes developing existing cooperation structures, initial and further training of employees in the field as well as quality assurance and evaluation.

⇒ The DPT feels that is necessary to have an age-specific, child and youth related understanding of violence as well as a narrow understanding of violence prevention. Only strategies aimed at programmes, measures, and projects which are mainly focussed on preventing or reducing violence during childhood and adolescence should be seen as violence prevention.

⇒ Establishing prevention strategies has focussed more attention on and led to an increased sensitivity for (potentially) violent behaviour in young people. Also the population at large, as well as youngsters themselves, are now displaying a stronger tendency to report incidents. These developments are part of a culture of "not turning a blind eye" and as such are to be welcomed.

⇒ However, an increased tendency to also report violent acts of a less serious nature - which used to go unreported in the past - might give rise to problems, particularly when informal conflict resolution gives way to earlier formal social control and when age-typical behaviour amongst young people is disproportionately categorised as unacceptable and might even be prosecuted.

Overall progress in youth crime in recent years

Generally speaking the level of exposure to crime, and particularly violent crime, is officially higher amongst young people as compared to adults. This has been observed for over a hundred years, i.e. since the advent of crime statistics. It holds true for Germany as well as other countries around Europe and places further afield, such as Northern America.

This is a basic observation which is valid over the long term and can be attributed, amongst other things, to processes of modernisation in society and their (sometimes undesired) effects. In the short and medium term, however, there may be uncharacteristic developments in crime figures and people's exposure to crime levels. Sometimes there are downward trends but there may also be perceivable upturns which usually lead to mounting concerns. The current situation can be described as follows:

⇒ In terms of crime reported in police crime statistics youth crime, as an overall phenomenon, is falling after a ongoing perceivable rise in the 1990s.

⇒ For certain types of crime, however, there is a continued upward trend in the number of officially reported cases. These include violent offences and, for the group of young people, assaults in particular.

⇒ Yet caution should be exercised when evaluating these seemingly obvious statistical findings: When we also include findings from studies of unreported crimes we can see that crimes committed by young people today are more frequently registered by the police than in the past and that, as such, behaviour deviating from the norm is indeed becoming more frequent amongst the younger generation. However this can also be largely explained by the aforementioned higher sensitivity of the population and the resulting willingness to report more crimes.

⇒ Findings from current empirical youth studies in various German regions and cities on self-reported delinquency (offender surveys) and self-reported victimisation (victim surveys) support this assessment.

⇒ Both offender and victim surveys show that depending on the area of study the level of violent crime amongst young people is either predominantly stable or even falling.

⇒ Having questioned several thousands of young people in Germany these surveys also showed that the propensity to violence is decreasing and that more and young people disapprove of violence.

⇒ As part of an overall assessment of the circumstances, the findings from both reported an unreported case data give no indication for a dramatic increase in the levels of violence or brutality amongst young people in Germany.

Youth crime is widespread

⇒ Reliable findings from national and international research show that delinquent behaviour amongst people might be widespread but that is mainly episodic in nature.

⇒ This means in concrete terms that for the majority of young people delinquent behaviour is only temporary and that it either corrects itself during a young person's development or with the help of interventions of people or institutions in their immediate environment.

⇒ This age-related phenomenon should therefore not be interpreted as an indication that most young people will continue to be long-term delinquents after they committed one or several offences.

⇒ Youth-typical delinquent behaviour of the majority of younger people is often linked to personal problems during their various stages of development, to conflicts in terms of finding out who they are and the resulting dissociation from parents and other educators, to getting used to becoming an adult and to peer pressure. It hardly ever has to do with grave behavioural disorders or educational deficits.

Serious youth crime is fairly rare

⇒ Only a small section of young people display long-term criminal tendencies linked to frequently committing serious offences.

⇒ These developments often start in early childhood and regularly point to considerable social as well as individual deficits and shortcomings.

⇒ Young people who frequently become noticed by the police over a period of time (so-called multiple and intensive offenders) display many risk factors. Protective factors are either missing entirely or are not available on time.

⇒ Crime statistics, youth study findings and practical experience show that this risk group of young multiple and intensive offenders mainly includes young males and particularly those with a migration background.

⇒ In these serious cases it is essential to show these young people where their limits are. This also implies quick responses as soon as possible after an offence has been committed. Serious interventions and long-term measures need to be tailored to the individual young person in order to be effective. To this end we recommend a multidisciplinary approach, e.g. case conferences which bring together youth and child services, the police, the prosecution service and the courts.

Conclusions:

Over time there have always been young people who have overstepped the mark, tested their limits, looked for adventures and sought recognition of their peer group. Norms have always been breached and crimes have always been committed.

⇒ Empirical findings do not necessarily confirm the public's perception that youth crime today is more frequent and youth violence more brutal than ever.

⇒ Neither studies of unreported cases nor any statistics by the police, the courts or otherwise, provide reliable pointers that there is a rise in brutality amongst young people across the board.

⇒ There is also no evidence for the widespread assumption that there is a perceivable ongoing rise in violence amongst girls or violence in schools. There are different reasons for the gap between public perceptions and empirical findings on youth crime and youth violence, one of the more prominent ones being media reporting. Media coverage tends to focus on spectacular individual cases which occur from time to time and which are unusual and, because of that, create a great deal of furore. Non-spectacular statistical findings regarding overall patterns do not necessarily make the papers. Over time this may lead to large parts of the population being under the impression that it is not just a few young people but a large number and increasingly bigger sections of children and young people who are turning to crime and violence and who are becoming more reckless and brutal than the young people of earlier generations. Particularly in troubled times such as these when the population seems to have so many different fears and concerns it is essential to reduce feelings of fear and threat when it comes to problem situations or young people deviating from the norm by having unbiased media coverage and balanced discussions.

For this reason the DPT considers it to be an ongoing priority for experts and those responsible in the field to keep referring to all available facts: facts regarding youth crime as well as facts regarding all the different ways and possibilities to effectively prevent delinquent behaviour by children and young people. These facts together with empirical data support the general diagnosis that trends are not as clear cut as is commonly assumed along the lines of: "ever more, ever worse, ever younger and ever more desperate". Certainly, practical experience shows that there are specific areas which give rise to concern and which need to be monitored diligently. These include the aforementioned multiple and intensive offenders but also integration issues for young people with migration backgrounds and the dangers posed by new media formats, by early drug and alcohol consumption and vandalism.

General developments in terms of youth crime might be favourable but they should not distract from the fact that in some cities and communities problem situations have arisen relating to certain areas or certain groups be they particular neighbourhoods, youth clubs or even schools. Here we need effective, integrated programmes of local crime prevention to be used as counter-measures.

The DPT calls on those responsible in the media and in politics

⇒ to take note of the positive developments in terms of youth crime
⇒ to support the educational tenor of initiatives and programmes in the area of crime prevention and
⇒ to promote the numerous cooperation efforts between the various fields of activity in the spirit of a generally accepted understanding of crime prevention.

The DPT feels it is vital that data on youth crime and strategies for the prevention of violence in the lives of children and young people are presented and discussed on a rigorously scientific basis and by drawing heavily on the experience of practitioners.

To this end DPT explicitly welcomes
⇒ the Periodic Safety Reports published by the German government and
⇒ the Report by the German Youth Institute based on a decision by the Conference of Prime Ministers of the *Bundeslaender* and drafted with the cooperation of the German Forum for Crime Prevention (*Deutsches Forum für Kriminalprävention*)and the Police Crime Prevention Units of the *Laender* and the Federal Government (*Polizeiliche Kriminalprävention der Länder und des Bundes*).

www.ingramcontent.com/pod-product-compliance
Lightning Source LLC
Chambersburg PA
CBHW070252290326
41930CB00041B/2460